LIFE WITH A SMILE
WYNETTE A. BRYANT

Library of Congress Cataloging-in-Publication Data

©2004 Wynette A. Bryant
ISBN: 1-4116-2667-2 (trade paper)

Cover design and photograph by Georgio Sabino III

Life With A Smile

Terri:

May God Continue to
Bless Your Life.

Enjoy your marriage
may let the honeymoon
end.

Keep Smiling
Agretta
9/10/05

PREFACE

These are the writings of my life as I remember it. I am sure that upon reading it there will be some that disagree with my perception and I am fine with that. I must write as I saw, felt and experienced.

To my parents, Carl and Catherine Bryant, thank you for loving me unconditionally and teaching me about love and forgiveness. To my little sisters, Celeste, Constance (Kayce), Christina (Chris or Tina), Janna (J), Lydia (Lay-Lay), I love you all more than life will ever allow me to express. I would give my life for anyone of you. To my children, LaToya and Archie, I am sorry for the mistakes I have made and the ill effects they may have had on your lives. Please know that all my mistakes were made out of ignorance and love. I would give you both the world if only it were mine to give. To my grandchildren, Devon and Nya, your Gran loves you!! Devon, you are and shall eternally be the best Boo in the whole wide world! Nya, you are forever my Nya-Love!

In case you think I forgot you, think again. To my brothers, Carl, Jr. (Chuck), Carey and Christopher (Bookie / Bryan), I love you even when you feel that I don't. Carl, Jr., thank you for being a big brother when I needed one and just Chuck when I needed, Chuck. Carey, I pray for you. Bryan, you will always be my Bookie-Bear, I don't care how old you get or who else hears, you are loved!!!!

To my best friend, you know who are.... I won't mention you by name so that others will not be offended. But, you are my ACE; I would not have made it this far without you. Our love for one another will go with us to our graves and if God says the same I pray that I will meet you in heaven.

I am writing this book, in order to heal, grow and learn more about myself. I am not writing to hurt or to seek revenge. I am praying that someone will be helped, delivered and encouraged by my life's experiences.

INTRODUCTION

To be honest, I don't know if I should begin at the beginning of my life or at the point in life I find myself now. I will just begin to write and see where things go.

Let me introduce myself. My name is Wynette. I am in my early forties, but my story is twenty-six and I'm sticking with that. I am the oldest girl in the family of nine children, six girls and three boys, the mother of two, grandmother of two and possibly eternally divorced.

I have been married three times; yes, I said three times. My first born, one of the most beautiful, intelligent and dedicated women I have ever come to know was born of my first marriage to my high school sweetheart (referred to as High School Sweetheart or HSSH). My son, the only man in my life that I would give anything unconditionally, is multi-talented, energetic and Mr. Personality and was born out of wed-lock to the one man I can say most assuredly; I have loved and will forever love, Archie.

My second husband, the younger man I married in a whirlwind romance. (I will refer to him as younger man or YM.) No let's be honest, it was lust and a plea for my true love to stop me, but we will get to that later...

My most recent and last husband, unless God says otherwise, the pastor (referred to as Pastor).

So you ask, "Why did she begin with the men?" The majority of my life was dominated, damaged and/or in some way destroyed by men. Don't get me wrong, I am not writing to bash men. I love men. I am glad God created them. I know that there are some good one's out there. My father is an example of a wonderful man. I see his flaws, but his character is of God. My uncle, (Rob not related by blood but by heart), has his weaknesses but is a true displayer of unconditional love. My great-uncle, Jimmy, God bless him, is just, what can I say, Uncle Jimmy. Archie, not my son, his father, with all his *friends*, is a true friend.

2

So, why do I feel that men have wreaked so much havoc in my life? Maybe, this is where I should begin.

I do not remember my birth, although I have been told that I was born on a Monday, at 8:48 pm on the twenty-seventh day of August in Lancaster, Pa. Here is where things really get fuzzy. I know that I came in weighing an even six pounds and I was nineteen inches long. These facts are in writing, it is the other stories that I've heard that I am not sure if I believe. My natural mother, you know the woman who gives birth, told me that I was a dry birth. Okay, I will explain, the after birth or placenta came first than the baby, me (?). I had blue blood and had to have a blood transfusion at birth (?), okay. And, I was her independence, makes sense to me, NOT! Well what she meant was that she was naming me whether my father approved or not. (In case you missed it in my preface, the names of five of the first six children born in my family all begin with the letter C, the sixth, the first born girl, that would be me, Wynette.) So for the first sixteen years of my life, I felt like an outcast. I cannot place all the blame on Jean (birth mother), my parents continued the saga with my younger sisters, until I pleaded with them to please give my next sibling a name beginning with something other than the letter C.

I'm sure you are somewhat confused at this point so I will back track for a moment. My father has been married twice, his first wife, Jean, gave birth to my two older brothers, one younger sister and me. They were divorced for reasons I will leave unmentioned and my father met and fell in love with my mother. My parents then gave birth to four more daughters and adopted a son. Our home was always full of love, laughter and children. My parents fostered and raised and helped to rear many children.

Having so many children in one house can be a blessing and a curse. When there are so many kids in the house, it is not always easy to know what they are doing or what's being done to them. But, we always had plenty of unconditional love.

So, I have given you the facts. Now I guess, I will begin with the first divorce of my life.

CHAPTER ONE

My father and birth mother were divorced when I was six months old. My father was the custodial parent of my two older brothers and me. My younger sister was in the custody of our birth mother (she was still pregnant with her at the time of the divorce and said that she would swear in court that this child was not his). Oops, I guess now you know why they were divorced.

My father had the assistance of his parents in caring for my brothers who were one and two years old at the time, but a baby just was too much for them. My father decided that his first cousin, who to him was more of a sister was probably the best place for his precious baby girl and she happily obliged. So my first memory of a mother was that of my second cousin, Lois, who became known to me as, Mom and later in life as Aunt Lois. (To be honest, in the presence of my mother, she's Aunt Lois, in my mother's absence she's Mom. But my mother is aware and doesn't mind sharing her title.)

My Aunt Lois cared for me until I was about two years old and then felt that her attachment to me was too great. She knew that my father would never allow her to adopt me and she knew he would one day remarry, so she returned me to my father and grandparents.

I did not realize at the time, but later I came to learn that I developed somewhat of an attachment disorder, because during the times in early life that I should have bonded the bonds were abruptly broken.

Now what is a two-year-old girl to do in a home with a working father and grandfather, a very busy grandmother and two very rambunctious brothers? Visit with the next-door neighbor, who showered her with love and affection.

Mrs. Dolly was white, her husband was black but I did not notice this and it wasn't important to me. I only mention it now because they were a happily married inter-racial couple before it was ever considered okay. Visiting with them was the beginning of my troubles although I did not come to realize it until I was an adult.

4

Mrs. Dolly's husband had been married previously and had older children. One of his older children, a son, would take me out to the shed, put my hand in his pocket make me feel around until I found something hard, cylinder in shape and throbbing and then ask me what I was feeling. How would a two to three-year-old know what they were feeling?

Then he instructed me not to tell anyone and would give me candy, a Popsicle or money and send me on my way. Some may think that wasn't so bad, but to those of you that are survivors of sexual abuse, you know better. This conditioned me not to tell.

By the time I was four-years-old, my father had met and proposed to my mother. My mom was young (21) full of energy and overflowing in love. My first real memories of a relationship with God began with my relationship with my mother. (I have to stop here, just to thank God for the blessing he sent me, in my mother. Thank you, Jesus!!!)

Mommy took us to church, in the cold, in the heat, during the week and always on Sunday. Mommy took us to school. She cooked for us and put treats under our plates at dinnertime. Well, that was until my brother, Carey, decided to put a treat under Mommy's plate – a spider.

I remember my first day of school. I did not want to go. I did not want Mommy to leave me. I was afraid she would never come back. (Why should she my other two mothers didn't)? It seemed as though Mommy understood, I remember her sitting in the back of the classroom to encourage me to stay. I remember the day I turned around and she was not there, I cried until she returned at the end of the day. I would not speak to the teacher or the other students. Then one day, I realized this Mommy, always comes back!

CHAPTER TWO

Mommy was from Cleveland (Ohio) and living in a small town like Columbia (Pennsylvania) became unbearable after a couple of years, so Daddy agreed that we should move to Cleveland. By now, I was starting the first grade and was well adjusted. I was truly settling in and feeling free in my newly found love.

Church in Cleveland was much better than the one in Columbia. Guess what? There were women preachers and the pastor was my new grandmother. I loved the music. This was a lively church; you could clap, sing and even do a Holy dance. Finding love in my mom made it easy for me to find love in God.

I found God in my early childhood. I was filled with the Baptism of the Holy Ghost at the age of seven. I really liked the feeling I got from attending church. I couldn't wait to go. We would travel to different cities and states to church assemblies and programs. I was building friendships all across the country, many of which have lasted to this day. I was comfortable, maybe too comfortable.

Somewhere along the way, I do not remember when or where and I really don't want to remember. My older cousin, the son of my mother's sister, began to sexually molest me. At family gatherings, sleepovers, in the car, closet wherever he felt sure not to be found out, he would fondle, touch, kiss and whatever else he chose to do to me. This all began at the ripe old age of seven. (Remember, I was already conditioned not to tell.)

What made this situation worse was that he was having problems at home with his stepfather and he needed to move out. My mom, with her heart of gold, could not fathom her nephew in the cold streets and took him in. Mommy was a nurse that worked nights in the children's ward of the hospital. Daddy was a laborer that left for work at four o'clock in the morning. So I was awakened nearly every morning (night to me) with an overweight teenager baring down on my underweight and small framed seven-year old body.

This disgusting activity continued until I was fourteen-years old. I can remember pinning my pajamas together. I only wanted pajama's that zipped up – you know the kind with the feet in them like babies wear. If I had to have the other kind it had to be tops and bottoms so I could pin them on me. I would have pinned them to my flesh if I could have. I never wanted gowns or the pretty kind, God forbid; he might think I was encouraging him. I prayed, I cried but I never told.

I begged God to make him stop. For God sake he was a Junior Deacon in the church. As I got older and understood how babies were made, I begged God not to ever let me get pregnant by him if He wasn't going to make him stop. He got married. This should make things better. Think again, when he was asked to baby-sit and his wife wasn't watching, guess who was the object of his affliction. Yes affliction not affection.

My prayers were finally answered. He stopped and just when my mother was becoming overwhelmingly concerned that I was approaching my fifteenth birthday and I had not yet started to menstruate. (Thank you, Lord!) A week before my fifteenth birthday, I began my first period.

In between my seventh and fifteenth birthdays, I have now come to realize that he was not my only abuser. The other is already deceased and victimized two of my sisters as well. I live with the guilt of not telling. Could I have prevented their pain? God knows if I knew then, what I know now, I would have told. I would have screamed it from the highest mountain…**STOP!**

I remember, I remember the smell, I remember the embarrassment, I remember the pain, and I remember the sick feeling. I remember the feeling of betrayal. I remember the guilt. The guilt, yes the guilt. Fornication is a sin. I hear it all the time. Having sex outside of marriage is a sin. If you are having sex with some one that is not your husband or wife it is adultery and it is a sin. But, I am saved. I have the Baptism of the Holy Ghost! I know that I do! I can feel God moving in my life. I can feel God's call on my life. How can this be if I am sinning?

I acknowledged God's call to the ministry at the age of twelve. I preached my first sermon about a month and half later on Labor Day Sunday at the age of thirteen. Imagine that, I am a preacher. I am twelve-years old called to be a vessel of God and I am having sinful, painful, shameful sex. I thank God that prayer really does change things. I now know that fornication and adultery are willful acts. I know that forced sex, rape and molestation are sins against you and not sins you are guilty of. But that little girl was confused!!! That little girl, who loved church and God, hated God. It's painful to admit, but I hated God almost as much I loved and wanted to please him. Is that even possible?

God, I am yours, your chosen vessel. You said, "Touch not my anointed and do my prophet no harm." Then why won't you make him STOP! What have I done to displease you? What did I do to make him want to touch me this way? What do I have to do to make him leave me alone? If God doesn't hear me does anyone hear me? So I carried this guilt and uncertainty into my adult years and yes into my marriages.

CHAPTER THREE

Aside from the secret of my abuse, I would say that I had a pretty normal childhood. As you are already aware, I have a lot of sisters. To say that I love my sisters would be an understatement. I felt as though they belonged to me. I remember the first day each of them came home from the hospital. That is with the exception of Celeste and Lydia.

I don't remember Celeste coming home because, I was only a year old and she was with Jean; while at that time, I was with Mom Lois. At the time of Lydia's birth, I was married for the first time and living in Nashville, TN.

You cannot imagine the joy I received from these beautiful little angels Mommy and Daddy called my sisters. Each one of them had locks of jet-black hair. Some had curly hair, some straight but they all had lots of hair. I had the time of my life diapering and feeding, holding and cuddling. Who needs dolls when you can have the real thing? Was I jealous, not ever, that I can remember. I had nothing but love for these bundles of love.

As much as I loved them, I had this overwhelming fear of losing them. I had anxiety attacks from wondering what would happen if something ever happened to my mother. I was young enough to enjoy playing with them but old enough to realize that Mommy was their birth mother and not mine. I knew that Mommy had never legally adopted my older brothers and me. I was afraid.

Some might ask what was there to be afraid of. I had a Mom, I mean a real Mom. I had the kind of Mom that would tuck you in at night or read you a bedtime story. I had the kind of Mom that listened to you when you talked and just let you sit in her lap just because it was empty. (Believe it or not, I still do if the opportunity presents itself.) I had the kind of Mom most children only dream of. But if something ever happened to my Dad, what would happen to my older brothers and me?

This was almost too much for a young child to live with. It was a constant fear, if Daddy came home late. Or God forbid, they would argue. "Lord, please don't let them get a divorce, I love my Daddy, but I need my Mommy." I remember praying this prayer so much. If something did happen to Daddy, would we be forced to go live with Jean, we don't even know her. To be perfectly honest, I don't even like her. The very sight of her makes me sick to my stomach. And she always wants to touch me, why?

Then there is Mommy's family. I love my aunts and uncles. Most of my mother's family is very loving and supportive, but every family has that one. My one aunt (God rest her soul) was all about **blood** family. She made it her point to make that clear. What if something happened to Mommy? Would they separate me from my sisters? They are mine! I will fight to the death for us to stay together! (Imagine, all of this going through the mind of a child.)

This aunt of mine, made certain to remind me that I wasn't as beautiful as other people told me I was. She would say, "You're not that pretty. If you were Hollywood would have discovered you by now. After all they came to Cleveland to find Jane Kennedy." She would say things like, "Don't think you have good hair because it hangs down your back that stuffs hard to tame. If you've got hair it's good. If you don't it's bad." And to think it was her son that was sexually molesting me. So, she gave the verbal, psychological and emotional abuse and her son killed me from the inside out.

Enough about that back to my beautiful, gorgeous, outrageous sisters. I remember the relief I felt on my eighteenth birthday. I knew that at this point if anything horrible were to happen to my parents. I was old enough to take care of them myself and now no one could ever take them away from me. I guess you might be wondering, are they still close? I think that the television series, SISTERS, opening slogan said it best, "From the cradle to the grave you will always have your sisters!" Or as my sister, Celeste, would say, " from the womb to the tomb we are sisters."

Now don't get confused. That doesn't mean that we don't have our spats, but don't you ever try to get in. (Just ask the husbands.) We are sisters to the death. We might fight amongst ourselves, but we will not allow anyone, not even our children to speak harshly against our sisters.

And if you ask any of us on any given day who our best friend is, nine out of ten times the answer will probably be, my Mommy. That's right we all take possession of her. We all think she belongs individually to each of us. We might share her, but she is each of ours separately as well.

Now about Celeste, if you were paying attention, you probably remember that Jean raised her and not Mommy, so how does she fit in? Like a bug in a rug, she's our sister. We spent a few summers together as we were growing up, but it was always a strained relationship. In my opinion, Jean was jealous of Mommy. I never quite understood that. She did not want us, but she did not like our relationship with our Mom. It puzzles me to this day. Rather than undermine or be hateful, why not be grateful that this woman took in your children and raised and loved them as her own? To me it is like adoption; if you did it for the right reason, let go. Hope for the best and be thankful for good adoptive homes.

Anyway, when I turned eighteen, I made a point to contact my sister. I expressed to her that they may have been able to keep us apart as kids, but as adults it was up to us to build a relationship and we did. (From the Womb to the Tomb!) By then, Celeste had already had her first child, a beautiful baby boy. I was married and expecting my first child.

CHAPTER FOUR

I loved school as I remember it. I was a pretty decent student. In hindsight, I must have been as much as perfectionist as a child as I am as an adult. My transfer from the schools in Columbia, Pennsylvania started with a fight. This was not my fight it was Mommy's. (Mommy has always stood up for us, no matter what she may have had to endure, that is, as long as she believed she was right or we were being treated unfairly. The catch twenty-two was we had better been telling the truth or that same zeal used to defend us would be used to chastise us.)

The Cleveland School Board had the policy of putting the children back a grade if the curriculum of the other district did not measure up to their standards and they wanted us to go back a grade. Mommy said, "No, these kids are bright, give them a chance, see how they do. If they can't keep up after a semester, I'll agree to them repeating a grade." Of course, that never happened.

By the end of my first school year in Cleveland, I was recommended to attend Enrichment Classes. These were accelerated classes that challenged the brighter children and introduced them to a foreign language. It was the belief of the country; it seemed at that time, that with our close relationship with Canada, Americans needed to know how to speak French. So my foreign language classes began in the third grade.

I took French classes from the third through the tenth grades. I spoke it fluently, I could read and understand it. By the eleventh grade we were to read novels in French. I decided that I'd had just but all the French I could take and opted not to take French in the eleventh grade. (The real reason, I didn't want to take French in the eleventh grade was that, I had a difficult time translating the novels in French. You see, although I was reading French words, I heard the English translation in my head. When it came time for testing, I had a difficult time translating the English back into French. Weird, huh?)

I poured myself into my class work and into my church activities. I had to distract myself from the night terrors some way. (Statistic show that most children of sexual abuse normally act out and grades drop. I internalized everything. I was always trying to figure out what I could have done differently to make things happen differently. I still do this in many aspects of my life. My Mom says I am my own worst critic. She is probably right, she usually is.) So my grades soared. I had awards on top of awards. I was inducted in the National Junior Honor Society and the National Honor Society.

After being inducted into the National Junior Honor Society in the eighth grade my school counselor suggested to my parents that I go to private school. She explained to my parents that I would be tested and if I performed well, I could receive a scholarship to attend. I was tested on Saturday, May 22nd, from 9:00 am until noon. You guessed it, I aced those test and received a one-year full scholarship. Tuition costs were about the same as college at the time, so when my scholarship award check mysteriously disappeared for the tenth grade, I returned to public school.

I loved to write. I usually wrote notes to people that I never gave to them. Oh, I had ways to let out my anger and if anyone had ever read my letters, I probably would have received the spanking of my life. Oh get real, yes, I got spankings. It wasn't the spankings that damaged me; some of them most likely saved my life. It is society that is so twisted about discipline. Explain this to me, why is it wrong and in some cases illegal to spank a child's behind in order that they might learn a lesson, but okay for a police officer to hit that the same child in the head with a Billy Club to subdue him into an acceptable behavior. Isn't there something wrong with that picture?

Anyway, I wrote. I wrote poems, letters and songs. I wrote when I was happy, but mostly I wrote when I was angry. And I was really angry. I wrote for sermons. I wrote speeches. I wrote for assignments.

(In case you are wondering how I arrived at the title for this book, it is from my tenth grade final writing assignment. I had to write an autobiography. I wrote it in third person using the pseudonym, Sheri Lowe and titled it <u>Life With A Smile</u>. It was on the first page of my scrapbook from high school, which I found approximately three years ago, and the closing statement brought me to tears. The insight into my own soul at such a young age was frightening. It reads, "Life has not always been a "bowl of cherries", for Wynette but her remedy is a smile. She has often said, "Smile, it's cheap medicine". Wynette does not always feel as happy as she may seem, but her smile usually covers her innermost feelings. She wants to leave this world with a smile on her face and she wants the world to smile when she's gone, because it really is the cheapest medicine.")

I was always great at the writing but the delivery whether by speech or mail that is where I cowered. I did not want to hurt other people's feelings. I did not want anyone else to ever feel what I was feeling inside. I did not want to do to others what was being done to me. So of course, since I would never speak up for myself, I was constantly being taken advantage of or teased.

The children in school called me, "white girl." My skin complexion is very fair and the grade and length of my hair I am sure didn't help my case much. So they would pull my hair, push me around and call me white girl. I would return home crying and my brothers would tell me that if I didn't learn to fight back that they were going to beat me up. They said every time I came home crying, they would give me a real reason to cry.

This is when the weight lifting began. By the time I was in the tenth grade and weighing eighty-five to ninety pounds, I could bench press a hundred and twenty-five pounds. (Today, I don't think I could bench press twenty pounds and I won't tell you what I weigh.) I had two and half fights while in public school. How do you have a half of a fight you might ask? Well I saw the schoolyard bully charging for me at full force as I was sitting on the guardrail in the playground. Just as he reached the point of contact, I got up and he went head first across the rail and into the gravel. Needless to say, he never bothered me again. (I told you I was a thinker.)

My other two fights were in the fifth and seventh grades. The first fight was with a girl and the last with a boy (who later in life became a girl – go figure). I didn't start either of these fights, but I finished both of them.

Karen had been in a fight in the schoolyard with another girl and lost. Her cry knocked me to my knees in laughter and of course that turned her anger from her first rival to me. You know, it has to be easier to beat up the girl that never sticks up for herself than anyone else. It would be as long as you didn't touch me and she decided to hit me for laughing at her. Let's just say, all that I remember after that was her lying on the ground, me on top of her and my fist repeatedly finding her face. The other kids saw the principal coming; they pulled me off of her and everyone scattered. The most she did after that was give me dirty looks in the coatroom.

In the seventh grade, I was nicknamed the "Kindergartner". Why, you ask? Well the fact that I was still wearing a child's size 6X and eternally wearing two pigtails that reached my elbows may have had something to do with it. Well, this boy twice my size and most likely three times my weight decided to pull my hair and jump on my back. Why? I don't know. All I know is that after I beat the crap out of him, I went to the basketball court, where my big brother, Carl, Jr. (a ninth grader) was. I was crying like crazy when I told him what happened. His buddies could not believe that anyone would ever mess with the "Kindergartner" and this poor fellow got the beat down of his life.

In high school, I got plenty of threats, but no one ever reached out to find out what I was made of. I'm really thankful of this because by then my rage could have been quite dangerous. Most of the fight threats were due to my high school sweetheart. I must admit he was the best looking guy in school and smart. He could miss school all week, come to school on Friday take the test and get A's. As much as I admired him, I also hated him. I had to work hard for my A's and B's and he could just take a test. (What a crock!)

He was my heartthrob. We were virtually inseparable. We had made our wedding plans and set the date, March 22nd, the year after graduation. The teachers went on strike during our senior year prolonging our graduation to July. By the time we graduated, I was pregnant with a due date of, you guessed it March 22nd, so our wedding date changed to September 19th, his eighteenth birthday.

Life With A Smile

I spent less than a quarter at Cleveland State University, when my Psychology Professor informed me that the only acceptable reason for missing the mid-term exam would be death. I politely explained that my baby was due during that week and his was reply was, "sounds like a personal problem to me." So I dropped out of college and with the exception of correspondence classes through my church and a childcare correspondence course, I have never returned.

CHAPTER FIVE

HSSH's dream was to go to school for the Music Business, so we followed his dream. There were three schools in the country that offered degrees in Music Business at that time; they were in New York, California and Nashville, TN.

We decided that New York was too crowded. California was too far away so we packed up and headed to Nashville. I was comfortable with the decision to move to Nashville. I had visited Nashville yearly since I was seven for our national church convention. I had friends there; I thought this would be a great adventure.

So we loaded up my parent's huge white fifteen-passenger van and headed south. As we traveled down 71S to 65S, I began to realize that my Mom and my sisters would not be coming with me. Mommy drove me to Nashville but she was pregnant too, with Lydia. I think this is when panic began to sit in. I think I sobbed quietly. We arrived in Nashville, unloaded the van into one of the dorm rooms on the church grounds, which I would call home for a few months, and Mommy got back in the van to return to Cleveland.

I had cried silently for as long as I could and I stood there in the parking lot of the church crying, sobbing and screaming to the top of my lungs. "No Mommy, I don't want to stay don't leave me!" With tears in her eyes, Mommy said, "Now, Nette, this is your husband, you will be fine. I will call you when I get home." With that she gave me a huge hug and gentle kiss on the cheek, rubbed the top of my head and told me that she loved me and got into the van and drove away. As she drove away she shouted to HSSH with tears in her eyes, "Boy, you better take good care of my baby!"

We moved into our first apartment when I was about six months pregnant. HSSH was going to school and had found a job in a group home for the mentally and physically handicapped and I had an office job at the headquarters of the same company.

My close attention to detail and good grades in my high school Accounting/Bookkeeping/ Computer Lab courses during my junior and senior years paid off. I had a trade, so while my husband went to school full time I was able to support our family. We had an agreement, he would go to school for four years and get his degree than he would work while I went to school and got my degree. It sure sounded like a great plan.

By the time LaToya was born her due date had changed three times with a final due date of March 16th. LaToya was two and half weeks over due when I went for my normal Wednesday weekly visit. The doctor informed me that he was sending me up to labor and delivery and that I was having my baby that day. I called my husband at school and told him what was going on and asked him if he was going to come to the hospital. His reply was no. Okay, it was April 1st, maybe he thought I was playing a joke on him or maybe he was just joking with me. He continued, "I have one more class today, I will be there after that." So I went to labor and delivery and I was induced.

I had pleaded with the doctor to let me go home. I did not want to have my baby on April Fools' Day. He insisted that I had to have the baby that day. I promised I would come back at 8:00 the next morning, 6:00 if I had to. He said, "No, today."

After having the IV with the medication for inducing birth running through my veins for about five hours, I asked the nursing assistant to remove the IV to see if I would labor on my own. (I was determined not to have my baby this day.) She said she would check with the doctor and after being unable to find him, she reluctantly agreed to remove the IV. Just as I was getting what I wanted the doctor walked into the room and said, "What are you doing? She is having that baby, today!"

I had gone up to the maternity ward at about 11:00 am, my call to HSSH was right before I left the clinic. He arrived at the hospital at or around 7:00 pm. (Where he was or what he was doing, I do not know even to this day. He said he had one more class. Perhaps that class lasted eight hours.) He arrived in enough time to suit up and join me in the delivery room. Fortunately for him, he put on the surgical clothing over his street clothes, because I grabbed his wrist and tried my best to break his skin with my grip. He may have thought it was a contraction, it wasn't it was rage. She came in weighing six pounds, thirteen and half ounces on Wednesday, April 1st at 7:26 pm. She was beautiful and she was perfect. I renamed April 1st, April Angels' Day.

During my pregnancy, I had refused to preach. I basically punished myself. I knew that I had sinned (this time it was a willful act) in conceiving my child and I did not want to anger God by acting otherwise. If my memory serves me correctly, LaToya was nearly a year old the first time I returned to the pulpit.

Being a wife and mother was harder than I thought it would be. I had helped with my little sisters but helping and doing it all was different, I quickly learned. I thought I knew all there was to know about baby girls. (Did I forget to mention, I prayed for a girl, I would have had no idea how to care for a boy's private parts.) I had helped Mommy with three little sisters by this time. I thought this would be easy, but babies don't sleep through the night and I cannot sleep during the day, so for the first three months of my daughter's life I was a zombie.

HSSH, didn't understand, why I could not attend to his needs and care for the baby and I thought I was going to lose my mind. I tried to lie down during the day, when she would nap but I just could not sleep it did not matter how tired I was. I need complete darkness, a closed door and complete silence. (Side effects of the abuse. If the door was open someone could enter the room without me knowing. If there wasn't complete silence I might not notice the breaking of the silence by a creaking floor or whatever else. I can't explain the darkness; I just need darkness.)

I began to feel resentment towards HSSH, he had a life and I felt he was denying me one. He was jealous and possessive. He didn't want me to wear shorts or tank tops, because he didn't want other men to see what he had. He didn't want me to play basketball with the guys, because it wasn't something girls should do. I had played ball with the boys all my life. I have two older brothers remember, we played basketball in our backyard with all the neighborhood boys. (Angie and I could beat any two on two team we played and we were always first picks on teams.) I played tackle football until the day I caught the ball in my chest and it hurt. I climbed trees to higher branches than any

19

boy. I even had a T-shirt that read, "I can beat any boy." Now all of a sudden, I am forbidden to be me.

I had not revealed my secret to HSSH. When the baby was nearly a year old we moved into a larger apartment. One evening in play, HSSH grabbed me by wrist and held me down on the bed. I began to cry and as politely as I could between gritted teeth I said, "Let me go." He laughed thinking he had gotten the best of me and held on tighter. Once again, I said, "Let me go", a little louder and with just a bit more force. By the third time, I had lost myself, with the next, "LET ME GO!" I gave a gigantic sigh and push. The next thing I knew, he was picking himself up off the floor and wall from across the room. I had to explain. How would he react?

HSSH was understanding and nonchalant at the same time. He said he would be careful not do that again, but I don't know if he was capable of handling what I had just loaded on him. My frustration in my marriage continued and was enhanced by HSSH indecision in his educational endeavors. He was taking courses towards his major rather than the required courses and changing his major constantly. By his third year, he had been on the National Deans list at least three times but was only an upper class sophomore. When he changed his major to Psychology, I suggested we go back home to Cleveland. There was no longer a reason to remain in Nashville if he wasn't studying the Music Business. He agreed and we started making arrangements to return to Cleveland.

As the breadwinner of the family, my daughter and I left for Cleveland first. I stayed with my parents while looking for a job. It didn't take long until I found a job in the corporate accounting department of major jeweler in the downtown Cleveland area.

By the time HSSH had finished his quarter in school, I had rented the downstairs of a two family house and life was better for me. But I did not want to be with my husband, I was enjoying the separation.

Upon arriving in Cleveland, he enrolled at Cleveland State University and found a part-time job. Shortly after his return, I received a better job offer at a health insurance company and I took it.

20

My new job required a lot of overtime and we did not have a car. The walk from the bus stop to the house was almost four blocks and HSSH began to complain that he did not think it was safe for his wife to be out all hours of the night. (Then perhaps, he should have gotten a better job or a second job.) To cut down the confusion my supervisor offered to drop me off in the evenings when I had to work late. I discussed this with my husband and he thought it was a great idea, that is, until he met my supervisor.

He was an attractive slightly older man and apparently a threat to my husband. Honestly, at the time I had never given him a second thought. I did not like him. I thought he was arrogant, self-centered and a womanizer. But in some ways, he became the beginning of the end of my marriage.

I was frustrated, not just with my husband. I was frustrated with life. I began a downward spiral. I was headed for disaster and this time I could only blame myself. I wanted out of this facade of a marriage. I wanted my turn to go to college. I wanted my life back and with the exception of my child, nothing made me happy.

HSSH began accusing me of having an affair with my supervisor. I tried to get him to understand that if I had been some where other than work my paycheck would reflect it. He insisted that there had to be more to my relationship with this man and the more I denied, the more he accused. I began to confide in my supervisor the problems I was having at home and he felt it best to stop giving me rides home. (Always the gentleman.)

I left him. I went to my parents' house and every night for a week, he would show up at my parents and slept on the couch. At the end of the week my Mom approached me as I headed out for work and said, "Nette, your husband loves you, it is obvious, he's been sleeping on the couch every night just so he can be where you are, go home, baby, go home."

You must remember, at this time I was not good at expressing what I was feeling. I never told anyone the things he had done to me; like complaining because I bought a pair of slacks off the clearance rack and got my hair done the same day. He said I was frivolous and uncaring. He said I was selfish and unconcerned about his needs and needs of our daughter. How dare, the man that left the house every morning to go to his part-time job before school that he had quit three weeks earlier, say these things to me. This is what I heard from the man that I was supporting and putting through college. This from the man that only bought his clothes from the designer men's store and had the best of everything at my expense. As for our daughter, she was the best-dressed child in the church and daycare. I had not even had a new pair of shoes for four years. Why was I sacrificing so much? I had endured more than enough.

I took a trip to Alexandria, VA, after HSSH left on his own. I took his older brother with me. While there a childhood friend of mine from Baltimore came to visit me at my cousin/brother's house (the son of Mom Lois) and stayed the night. It was totally innocent but I knew what it looked like and that was what I wanted. Of course, when we returned, his brother reported what he thought had occurred and HSSH agreed to grant me my divorce.

Previously, whenever I brought up divorce, he would threaten to fight for custody of our daughter. When I requested financial assistance from him, he would say, "If I can't have you, I don't want either of you!" (I really wished he would make up his mind.) With all the custody threats, I went downtown and filed for custody of my daughter and explained that she had never been separated from me. Filing for custody afforded me child support. (I was granted $35 a week and until LaToya was 18 that was all I ever got.)

With the custody scare out of the way, I filed for divorce.

Four years, one month and sixteen days later on November 4th, I was granted my divorce and returned to my maiden name.

CHAPTER SIX

I was enjoying my newfound freedom a little too much. I started going out with Angie, my best friend from childhood. Angie and I were connected at the heart and hip; we justly earned the nickname "Double Trouble". It was rare to see one of us and not the other. I was going to nightclubs. I began to drink and I frequented the male strip clubs. (Okay, I said that I was going to be honest. I didn't say I was proud of everything I did.) I continued to party and I began to date. I began to distance myself from the church and my family. They would never agree with my current life style.

Remember the supervisor I was accused of having the affair with. He became my best friend and eventually the true love of my life, Archie. Archie and I had an on again off again type relationship. We knew each other too well. We were both used to having things our way or no way. We clashed and we loved it. When we were good together we were greater than great, but when we were bad together, ugly could not begin to describe it.

After about six months Archie and I moved in together. Well, the truth is my apartment complex heating unit was out, they would not fix it and I moved in with Archie, against his wishes, initially. Things were good for a while, but Archie had too many female friends that disrespected our relationship and Archie did nothing to put them in their places. Did this ever make me angry!

Archie was and is the confirmed bachelor. My living with him was cramping his style. He loved me, but he liked loving me from a distance better. Shortly, after our moving in together, Archie lost his job. Another insurance company, out of California, bought out the insurance company we worked for and they were laying off management. In a lot of ways this helped our relationship. We no longer had to keep it a secret at work and I no longer had deal with the things he didn't like from work coming home. Anyone who has ever dated, married or lived with his or her boss will understand what I mean.

One night in anger I loaded up my car, pulled my daughter out of her bed and I was leaving. I had no idea where I was going. I was just going. Archie stood in front of my car and pleaded with me not to leave that way. He assured me that we could work things out and if not he would help me find a place of my own.

One of the other problems with our living arrangement was that the building we lived in was an adult only building (you know back when it wasn't illegal) and I had a four-year-old daughter. Fortunately, she was a quiet four-year-old and we were never discovered. Then the bomb dropped. I was pregnant.

Being pregnant was a big problem for me. I was just at the point were LaToya would be going to all day kindergarten in a Montessori school and I was considering enrolling in college. I was on birth control, how could I be pregnant? Well let me explain it. First of all birth control is not full proof. Secondly, I was having some adverse reactions to the pill and the doctor prescribed some other medication to counteract the reactions. What he failed to explain was that I needed to use additional protection while I was taking the other medication.

Now I know what some of you are thinking. "I can't believe she is putting in a book for anyone to read that she didn't want her second child." My son knows this story and believe me, he knows without a single doubt, that his mother loves the very ground he walks on. So, shall we go on?

So I was pregnant. Archie wasn't very happy about this situation either. He was in his early thirties and had no children. Did I mention that he was eight years my senior? He felt that adults don't make mistakes. (In other words he thought I got pregnant intentionally to keep him. Now some women out there are stupid enough to do this, but not me, I was already raising one child on my own and had absolutely no intentions of raising another one. LaToya was supposed to be an only child.) How would we be able to hide a baby in our complex? Someone was sure to hear the baby cry. We would have to buy baby furniture, how would we get it in the building undetected.

24

Archie questioned paternity, remember we had an on again off again relationship and I dated other men when we were off. (Yes, even living together, after all we weren't married. This was my mind's frame. I hate to admit that I have slept with more men than I can number or name. It is only by the grace of God that I am AIDS free and other than after being raped have never had a sexually transmitted disease. Don't worry; we will get to the rape later.)

I had been completely faithful, so you know that I was enraged at the implication that this baby might not be his. I cried, I screamed, I yelled, I threatened abortion (like that would ever happen), and I was miserable. Archie packed his bags and went to California for a week. I went to the doctor, got my prescription for prenatal vitamins and told him I would see him when I was willing to accept the pregnancy. I cried for three months, and then I said, "Lord, let it be a boy, because I am never doing this again!"

On my first real visit to the OB-GYN, I explained to the doctor that I wanted my tubes tied on the day the baby was born. I was large during my pregnancy and the doctors thought that I might be carrying twins (they run in my family) so I had an ultrasound early in the pregnancy, there was only one baby, and I just had a lot of fluid.

CHAPTER SEVEN

Pregnancy has never been good to me. With my daughter I had all day sickness for the first trimester. With this baby, I was sick the entire pregnancy. I had so many false labors the hospital should have just kept me. I gained over 50 lbs which I carry to this day and I just wanted to get this baby's foot, head, elbow or whatever body part that it was out of my ribs.

Coincidentally, the baby's due date was March 16th (the same date LaToya was due). I have so many relatives with birthdays in March. Mommy's is the 11th and I have cousins with birthdays on the 15th, 19th and 25th of March. And Archie's birthday is also the 19th. Everyone wanted the baby to born on his or her respective birthday. This baby had its own plans.

Just like the first baby, this baby was late. No matter how sick I was getting, this baby liked it on the inside and had no desire to be born. I began to dehydrate and could keep nothing down and nothing in so once again I was induced.

My son was born Easter Sunday, March 30th, two days before his sister's fifth birthday. He weighed seven pounds and three ounces and although I loved him dearly, he was just plain ugly. I know that not many mothers will ever admit that their precious baby is or was ugly, but my son was anything but cute. He was pale and pasty (from being in there too long) and his nose was the biggest thing on his body. Thankfully, by the time he was three months old and he was drop dead gorgeous and a real lady-killer. His head had caught up with his nose, his color was a beautiful golden brown and did I mention that his birthmark was a beautiful patch of blonde hair in the center of his head where Alfalfa's personality was from the Little Rascals.

During the pregnancy, Archie and I could not agree on a name for this baby. We did not know the sex, although I knew I had requested a boy from God. We finally agreed that if the baby were a girl we would name her Catherine Evangeline. The name Catherine was after my mom and Evangeline after Archie's grandmother. A boy's name we just could not agree on. I liked Bryon Scott, Archie said, "no way." I said we could name him Archie Thomas, the third. He said, "What if he's not mine?" (Okay, here we go again and with my hormones raging, this man is taking his life into his own hands.)

The baby was here and I had three days to name him. His father had five days to sign his birth certificate so that he would have his last name. So I named him, Archie (III). Big Arch, as he became known, waited to the eleventh hour to sign the birth certificate and only after I threaten to change is name did he rush into the hospital to sign. (Since we were not married, if the hospital sent the records to vital statistics the baby's last name would have been changed to mine.) I told Big Archie that if the baby were going to have my last name, he most certainly would not have his first name.

Naming him Archie was the best thing I could have done. The older he gets the more he favors his father. He is my son, but if I must say so myself, he is fine.

Little Archie was a crier so we knew our days were numbered at the apartment complex and we began looking for a new place to reside. We moved together, and then we separated, we moved back in together and apart. This was a vicious cycle for years to come. Finally, we decided to live together but have our separate lives. Surprisingly, this worked for a while. But all good things must come to an end.

Big Archie found fault in every guy I dated. He didn't want them around the children, which I really didn't have a problem with. He didn't want me to stay out late (even when the kids were with relatives for the weekend). Basically, he didn't want to marry me. He was fine not having a sexual relationship with me (as long as he believed no one else was) but he wanted me to live as though we were a family.

Eventually we separated for good. That doesn't mean that we did not continue a relationship of some sort, but for the most part we were not a couple. We were parents that loved our children (yes, I said our) and were determined to do whatever necessary to raise them together to the best of our abilities. We agreed that our friendship, the basis of our relationship, was more important than our romantic involvement, so we fell back on our friendship and it has worked for years.

Life With A Smile

You should not believe for one moment that it always worked well. It didn't, but it always worked. When you love some one so deeply and you realize in all likelihood you will never be together, it messes you up in the head. I did stupid things to get his attention.

I dated dangerous men. I dated married men. I dated actors. I dated bar owners. I even dated men from my church. I may not have been attending and practicing my beliefs like I should have but I went enough and traveled enough that I was still able to catch the eye of those that were professing to be something they weren't.

So we have made it back to the problem, my problem.... men.

CHAPTER EIGHT

I find myself alone; the mother of two and wanting above anything else to be loved unconditionally for the person I am. The man that I am madly in love with has made it perfectly clear after three attempts to marry, that he just is not ready for that type of commitment and wasn't sure if he ever would be. Wounded again, the speed of my downward spiral accelerated.

I became a weekend alcoholic. My drinking started at the 5:00 pm, Friday and usually ended at 5:00 am, Sunday. When work ended, I would drop of my children at my aunts and the partying began. The alcohol helped me to mask the pain I was feeling. At this point in my life, I just wanted every hurt and pain to disappear. Earlier in my writing, I stated that I did not want to hurt anyone. That is not the complete truth. I did want to hurt men. I wanted them to want and desire me so that I could love them and leave them. (Yes, I know that this thinking was more to my detriment than to anyone else. But at the time this realization had not occurred.)

My, "I can beat any boy" attitude from my childhood was acted out in the worst ways in my early adult life. My philosophy was, "If men can do it, so can I." Why is it that a man that has slept around with many women is a stud but a woman that sleeps around is slut?

The truth be told, the man is just as much a slut or sleaze as the woman or women with whom he has slept. (If you are out there doing the same thing women, STOP! You are worth more than what is between your legs. And what is between your legs is the greatest gift you can give. Value yourself higher, recognize that you are a queen or at least a princess and insist on being treated as such. Most of us don't lose our virginity we give it or throw it away. Your virginity is a gift you can only give once, so why not give it to your husband on your wedding night?)

I was having the time of my life as I saw it. I was throwing parties that included at least two male strippers. The rule of the parties was whatever happens here, stays here, so I cannot say more about the parties. With all this *fun,* there was something missing. I just did not feel complete. I was masking my true feelings. I was accustomed to doing so.

I decided to slow down my partying. I would go out on Fridays but not on Saturdays, because I wanted to go to church on Sunday and I did not want to reek of booze. I started to date only one man at a time and I was struggling to do what was right.

On one of my trips to the doctor for my regular check up, I met a young man that worked in the parking garage. He seemed nice. My great aunt worked at the hospital and she had nothing but good things to say about the gentleman, so we started dating. I was determined to do things the right way so sex was not in the equation. I was really beginning to enjoy the relationship. We would watch the football and basketball games together. We watched movies or went out to eat and we would just talk. This was refreshing.

He called me, "Cuddles", because we just cuddled as we watched television. On New Years Eve, we had a late night dinner at a popular Chinese restaurant in downtown Cleveland. We returned to my home, I sent my babysitter home and we sat down to watch the ball drop. Sometime that evening something went drastically wrong. This gentle man I had been dating snapped. He raped me. Using my long ponytail as a weapon against me, he yanked my head back, ripped my clothes off, told me that I was too hung up on Archie and forced himself on me. As I struggled to break free, he stated that he would hurt my children if I woke them. Do what you want to me, but leave my innocent babies alone.

I coughed, I choked, I threw up when he left and of course I did the wrong thing. I took a long soaking bath in the hottest water I could stand. While soaking and crying, I called Archie and to the best of my ability told him what happened. Archie immediately came over and tried to convince me to go to the police. I decided to go the next morning but I only wanted to file a report without pressing charges. (Why, you ask? Remember I had not been a saint and I did not want my past brought up in court. My parents had no idea of all of my deviant behavior and I surely would not allow them to find out in a court of law.)

The police explained the procedures and the steps they would take if I wanted to make a complaint. I decided not to pursue him and I pray that he has not done the same to someone else.

Now, I was really going through some stuff in my head. It was bad enough that I had endured such horror in my childhood. Why couldn't I see the signs or was there something wrong with me. Would I eternally be the victim of every sexual predator on earth? I could not eat, I could not sleep, and I was having flashbacks. I was a complete and total mess and in spite of what I was going through on the inside, I went to work everyday and cared for my children. (Life with a smile!)

Sex was the last thing on my mind; in fact I thought I might never have sex again. I knew that I was leaning too heavily on Archie so I decided to handle things on my own. I happened to encounter one of the male friends from the past and we began to talk. (I had really liked this guy and had broken off my relationship with him when I discovered that he was married.) When our paths crossed this time he had been divorced about six months.

I spoke openly with him about my recent rape and expressed that I wasn't sure if or when I would be ready for a sexual relationship. He was very understanding. He would stay the night with me and just hold me so that I could sleep. I found great comfort in this and eventually, I trusted him enough to once again resume a sexual relationship.

I will refer to him, as Earl and you will understand later why I have changed his name. Earl was a county correction officer and did not work on Mondays. This was great because he would stay over on Sunday nights and take care of all of my business and his with the use of my car on his off day. My car was always clean and he was very attentive to my needs. (Maybe a little too attentive.)

For reasons I do not remember we eventually stopped dating and I moved on with my life. I was grateful to Earl for allowing me to heal and progress. Shortly afterward, I met and married my second husband, whose first name was the same as my first husband's. (Okay, you're thinking, she married two guys with the same name, what was she thinking? It is even weirder than you think. The first husband's birthday is September 19th; the second husband's birthday is September 17th.)

CHAPTER NINE

I had reached a point in my life when I knew it was time to go back to church and get myself right with God. I had one major problem. I knew that I could not live without sex and I knew that I could not devote my life to God and have sex outside of marriage.

Archie and I talked, but he was dating other women and in a "relationship" with someone. I was having a few financial problems and we considered moving back in together but marriage was not an option.

Angie and I went out to our favorite nightclub at the time and I met a very attractive younger man. We partied until the club closed and then went to the all night diner that happened to share the same parking lot. I was intrigued. I went home alone and YM and I met the next evening over dinner. I decided that I didn't want to go alone so I dragged Angie out with me and we went to a concert afterward. YM and I began a whirlwind romance that ended in marriage thirty-nine days after our meeting on the hottest day of the year in one of the Metro Parks on the fourth of July. It was a scorching 104 degrees.

Now, if you have been attentive to my writings, you will recall that the romance I am claiming was really a plea to get Archie to ask me to marry him. I was praying that he would at least ask me not to marry this man. He did neither, so I plunged in, after all, the wedding guests had arrived and this man claimed to love me. Maybe, I would learn to love him. I had no complaints in the bedroom but how long would that satisfy me?

Before we married, I was smart enough this time to express my past abuse and rape to him. I was not going to make the same mistake twice. I was also very expressive about the way I was raised. I informed him of my call to the ministry and explained although I was not attending church the way I should have and was not practicing the ministry, I knew that one day, I would return to that calling. ...I could feel it calling me back. I knew I would not be able to resist much longer.

He was okay with everything I told him. (I was secretly hoping this would chase him away.) He had just gotten a job with a soft drink manufacturer as a truck driver and things seemed okay. I said seemed. I later found out, that most of the information YM had told me about himself and his family were lies. (This man was living in his own little fantasy world.)

They were unimportant lies but lies just the same. His car was really his mother's. He was driving back and forth to Twinsburg (a suburb about 20 minutes away) every day to take his mother to work because she did not have a car. He spoke Spanish fluently and stated it was because his mother was Puerto Rican. His mother is of a fair complexion. She is a black woman, that has a multiracial heritage like most of us, but none of them are of Hispanic decent.

He decided that he could not deal with the racial tension on his job, so without finding another one first, he quit his job. The financial strain became too much for me so I dropped the insurance on my car and started catching the bus to and from work. Can you imagine paying a car note and catching the bus? As I was making this sacrifice, my considerate husband decided to go out to look for a job in my car and of course he had an accident. Could things get any worse? Now we have both lost our licenses and my registration was revoked.

My involvement in the church had deepened and I returned to the ministry in January of the following year. My husband felt as though I were ignoring him because I was attending church on Wednesday and Friday nights and all day on Sunday. In addition, I was attending state and national meetings. He expressed that I was always gone and he was always left at home. I explained to him that he was always welcome to go with me, but that was not what he wanted. He was tired of being stuck at home with no transportation (now whose fault was that?) and he wanted to go out and party.

I never tried to stop him from partying after all I met him in a nightclub, what else would I expect of him? I am not one of those people that believe you can fix up or change someone to fit into your plans. I just made it clear that I would not be going to the clubs with him and that I would prefer that he not drink or smoke in the house.

(When I did party, I never exposed it to my children and I did not want him to do so either.)

He found a new job doing some sort of investigative work (or so he said) and he seemed to like it. He still was not contributing to the household however. He was buying top of line stereo systems and whatever else made him happy. He was spending most of his awake time in the basement doing who knows what and when he wasn't in the basement he was doing his best to make me miserable. Ultimatums and threats don't go over well with me and YM did not seem to get that concept.

Within our first year of marriage I sought the aid of an attorney and began divorce proceedings. He begged me not to divorce him. He promised that he would be more considerate of the children's and my feelings. He vowed to start pulling his weight and promised not to try to stop me from attending church. I dropped the proceedings and things improved for a while.

If I didn't mention before, YM was five years younger than me, so the father thing was very difficult for him. My daughter was nine and my son was four when we married. Not only was it difficult for him to deal with the children, he had a real problem with the fathers. Things were getting pretty ugly again. I prayed and anointed his side of the bed. I asked God to save Satan or move him.

If I thought he was spending a lot of time in basement before, it got a lot worse after I anointed his side of the bed. The first night he tossed and tossed and tossed. The second night he just got up and eventually it seemed he just never came to bed. He was sleeping in a lounge chair in the basement. Then it happened!

YM explained to me that his job was sending him to Florida for a week to do some investigative work on one of their clients. He explained that he would need to pay for the trip in advance and that he would be reimbursed for all his expenses upon his return. He told me that he had found a package deal and that he would return home the day after Valentine's Day. (How convenient!)

Now keeping in mind that this man has difficulty with the truth and something just didn't feel right, I began doing some investigating of my own. My first act was to call his job and ask his supervisor for a telephone number to reach him in Florida (of course, I had a number to the hotel, this was a test). His supervisor's response was. "Why would I have a number to reach him? He's on vacation."

The second step would take some help. I enlisted the help of a male friend that was like a brother to me, who happened to be an Ohio State Peace Officer. He made a phone call to the hotel with me on three way and YM answered the phone in his usual non-business tone with a "What!" Now if he were really on business, I believe he would have been more professional in answering, don't you?

Finally, I checked into this package deal he got on his trip. The package included a rental car for the week. Now explain this, how was a man with no license going to rent a car? (Remember we both lost our license due to his car accident in my uninsured car.) So who was going to be driving the car?

Needless to say, I had too many unanswered questions and I'd had enough! I did not get a lawyer. I filed for the divorce myself. (I told you I was intelligent, show me once and I've got it.) I prayed, "Lord, if it is your will that I divorce this man, please allow him to come home sign these papers take his things and leave without giving me a hard time. If it is not your will, help me to accept your will and I remain in this marriage and continue to pray that you save his soul.

I called his mother. I expressed to her my concerns. I told her the actions I had taken and asked her to pick him up from the airport upon his return. I wanted him to get his things and leave and I did not trust him not to become violent. I explained that I had not only changed the locks but I had replaced the doors with steel doors (he had kicked in the door in past when we got locked out by mistake and I wasn't taking any chances). Don't get the wrong impression, he never touched me in the past, however, he did always carry a gun. He had been known to punch walls and I just was not willing to take a chance.

When they arrived at the house, he stormed in shouting that he did not appreciate me checking up on him. He snatched the papers from my hand, signed them like he wanted blood to come forth from them, grabbed his things and left.

I saw him twice after that day. There was one paper I had forgotten to produce that I needed him to sign, so we met for the signing and the day we were divorced. I am thankful that to this date our paths have never crossed. Once again, I was divorced, March 23rd, a little more than three months before our third wedding anniversary.

CHAPTER TEN

During the time of my second marriage, two of my younger sisters revealed that they had been sexually abused. They stated that they could no longer live in silence and felt that for the sake of their sanity they had to tell. What was most difficult to fathom was that one of their perpetrators was our own brother and the other was our now deceased cousin (not the one that victimized me for years, his younger brother).

I was in panic mode. First of all, my brother, our brother, how could this be? He and his wife use to baby-sit my children while I worked. Oh my God, could he have? Would he have? I had to know.

I felt that I had always had an open line of communication with my children. Being a victim of child sexual molestation I always spoke to my children about uncomfortable touching. I would ask them questions like: "If any one touched you, you would tell me wouldn't you? You would tell me even if they told you not to, wouldn't you? You know that you can tell Mommy anything, don't you?" And they both would always answer, yes to all of the questioning and then go back to playing.

I sometimes felt as though I was over protective and unnecessarily suspicious. Now I know better. You can never ask too many questions, but make sure to ask the right ones. After pulling myself together emotionally, as best as possible, I put on my happy face and began to question my children. We were all in the kitchen and I approached the subject as delicately as possible. I never mentioned what I had learned or my brother's name. I simply, as calmly as possible, asked has anyone ever touched you in your private parts or done anything to you that made you feel sad, scared or ashamed? Before I could get all my questions out, my son said, "Mommy that's nasty, NO!" My daughter just sat in silence. The kind of silence I know well. So I continued my questioning as cautiously as possible. "Has anyone ever touched you and told you not to tell me or they would hurt you or your brother or even me?" Still there was silence and now a bowed head. So I asked a few more questions. "Is there any reason why you would not tell me if someone hurt you?" Nothing, just silence and I think I saw a tear drop.

I was not handling this well. Please don't hurt my babies! I tried to remain calm but I could feel the anger and the heartache and the pain stirring up within me. Then I just let it out. "LaToya", I said, "this is a yes or no question! Answer me, has anyone ever touched you in an inappropriate way?" She yelled back with the tears in full stream and the snot running down her face, "Yes, Yes, Yes!" Okay, I had to remain calm for her sake and I had to ask one more question without revealing what I had just learned about my sisters, so I took a deep breath and I asked, "who?"

I was prepared for her answer, I was ready to call my brother and let him know that I had every intention of prosecuting him to the full extent of the law. I was ready for everything except, what I heard. She said, "Earl, I hate him, Earl did!" I said, in a tone that I'm sure looking back probably made her feel like I didn't believe her, "Who?" Once again she shouted, "Earl!"

I had to refocus, this wasn't about me, this was about helping her, but I had more questions? How? When? Where was I? Was this the right time to ask? Would there ever be a right time to ask? What do I do next?

When we read in the scripture that "God is faithful, who will not suffer you to be tempted above that ye are able; but will with the temptation also make a way to escape, that ye may be able to bear it" please know that doesn't mean that it will be easy to bear. God in all his wisdom knew that when I was partying and sinning and doing whatever, that I was not emotionally or psychologically capable of handling what I had just heard. I would probably have been writing this from my prison cell convicted of premeditated murder.

The man I had poured my heart out to, the same one that helped me heal after my rape had molested my child. My God, how could I be so blind? Did she show any signs? How could I have missed this? When did he have the opportunity? "Please, Jesus, just help me help my baby!"

I held her in my arms and we cried. I told her I was sorry. I told her how much I loved her and would have never allowed this to happen if I had known. I told her that she had done nothing wrong and this was not her fault. I told her she had nothing to be ashamed of and that she was a victim and not some one who sinned. I asked her if she wanted to prosecute him. She was eleven now, she understood what I was asking her and her response was "yes." Her exact response was, "Mommy, I don't want him to do this to another little girl. He is a bad man and he has to be stopped, he needs to go to jail."

After she went to sleep, I called my brother-friend, the Ohio State Peace Officer, and asked how I should proceed. He advised me to call the child abuse hotline and gave me the name of a specific officer to ask for, the next morning I did just as I was instructed.

The case came to hearing on September 20th. We experienced quite a bit of trauma while awaiting trial, but I will allow the victim impact statement we submitted to the court to express our ordeal:

VICTIM IMPACT STATEMENT

Your Honor, we have been asked to make a statement on how the events that have led to this appearance have affected our lives. This is very hard to do, because we are unable to find ways in which it has not affected our living.

We live in constant fear. (This is not to say that we have not had any enjoyment since these incidents occurred, but it has become extremely difficult to relax or put our guard down.) Since bringing this case before the court, our male Chow Chow puppy was brutally murdered. The six-month-old dog was removed from his leash, stabbed and left to bleed to death on our front lawn. Our home has been burglarized twice, on July 7, (year left off intentionally) **and again on August 14, in the middle of the night while we were asleep in the house.**

We are aware that we cannot prove that Mr. (Earl) was responsible for these actions; yet, we cannot help but believe that these events are somehow related to this case. Burglars normally don't want to

40

break in when someone is at home, and why are these break-ins at or around 4:00 in the morning? It would seem, that there is an ulterior motive, perhaps to shut us up!

We are aware that since Mr. (Earl) pleaded guilty to a lesser charge he will more than likely receive probation. We would honestly prefer that he obtain a jail sentence of no less than two (2) years. I would like to share with you LaToya's statement on his sentence:

"What I think should happen to this very cruel and disgusting man is, I think he should spend some years in jail, no less than 5, because there are people like him all over the world, and I don't think they should get away with the things they do to people!"

LaToya has unjustly been made to live with fear, guilt and shame. I do not feel that (Earl) should walk away with a slap on the wrist. He, as a County Corrections Officer, is supposed to uphold the law. He is supposed to set an example of a decent citizen, upright and just. His actions were deplorable according to LaToya's statement of the events:

"What happened was, he ... and in the morning after my mother would leave for work, he would start.... me. Every time he did this to me, he would tell me not to tell my mother because she might get jealous. I didn't tell my mother until a long time because I thought that he would try to hurt us. All I really thought about was the safety of my mother, brother and myself."

We have been victimized enough! It is now up to the court to determine the outcome of these events. Your Honor, if probation is given, we beg of you to give the maximum probation of five years. We would also like to request that a stipulation of the probation be that he makes no contact with us, our friends and family members directly or indirectly. This includes the constant contact of Mr. (Angie's ex-boyfriend and Earl's best friend) to Miss Angela. Mr. (Angie's ex-boyfriend) is still attempting to manipulate Angela into giving out information about our family and this case. We would like to request that Mr. (Earl) and his associates maintain a distance of no less than 100 feet if our paths happen to cross in public. This may seem extreme, however, the events of the past few months lead us to believe that there may be some type of retaliation.

We would like to take this time to say thank you for taking the time to read our statement and consider our request.

Respectfully Submitted,

Ms. Wynette A. Bryant
(Mother of the Victim)
LaToya (last name omitted for my daughters privacy)
(Victim)

Earl received the maximum probationary period of five years and a protection order was given to my daughter including the 100 feet distance clause.

CHAPTER ELEVEN

Being the rock of stability for my daughter was taking a great toll on me, but it wasn't about me. I just kept smiling and kept going. On the inside I was reaching the point of no return.

I was not sleeping. I was afraid to sleep. My home was broken into twice during the middle of the night. Our house was the last one on the street with an empty lot next to it. There was a large grape vine that hid the south side of our home and the burglar(s) were using this to their advantage. I had an alarm installed after the first break in but it didn't seem to deter them.

Our home was ranch style with the bedrooms on the north side of the house and the living areas on the south side. LaToya's bedroom was in the front of the house off of the living room. Archie's room was off the dining room in the middle of the house. My bedroom was off the kitchen in the rear of the house and the bathroom was behind my bedroom and the kitchen in the far rear of the house.

I am a very light sleeper so when I heard footsteps going back and forth through the house, I thought the children were just going to the restroom. That night my children, my youngest sister, my oldest nephew and my three-year-old niece were in my home. I assumed that they were taking turns going to the restroom and attempting to be quite so as not to wake me. After about what seemed like fifteen minutes of this I was fed up, so I leaped to me feet yanked open my bedroom door and came face-to-facemask with the burglar. I must have startled him because he took off through the back door, which he had opened after breaking in through the kitchen window and he was running with what looked like a screwdriver in his hand.

By the time the police arrived, the sun had risen and I could see what was left behind outside by this vandal. What I thought was a screwdriver was actually an ice pick that he left as a calling card in my back porch. My niece's Barney towel was lying in the driveway. Throughout the house were matches that had been dropped as he cased the house. What was worse was that all the children, except for my son, were asleep on the floor in the living room and he had strategically

43

dropped matches around their heads. (It frightens me to think just what he was about to do with the towel and ice pick to those children.) It was clearly a warning and I did not take it lightly.

Our dog had been killed about three weeks before the first break-in. After the second break-in (the guy never made it into the house, I heard the kitchen window open and ran out of my room screaming an hit the panic button on the alarm system) I took an ax to that grapevine. As I saw it, it was the grapevine or our lives so the grapevine had to go.

It took me two days and I had blisters where I thought you could not get blisters. But I won the war against that grapevine. I nailed my windows closed from the inside and I prayed. I prayed hard and I prayed a lot.

Big Archie stayed over for a few nights and slept on the couch or in the room with our son. But I knew that would be like playing with fire and I was concerned about the appearance of evil, so I told him we were okay and that he did not need to stay with us. I could not let him or anyone else know how terrified I really was.

I was having flashbacks of my molestation. On the rare occasions that I did fall asleep, I was having reoccurring nightmares. I was falling apart, I was falling fast and I was falling hard. I literally fell while walking down the street from shear exhaustion. I have the scar on my left knee to this day.

I was not ready for this. Someone please help me! Prayer is good. I know God is capable of anything but right then I needed to lean on someone tangible. I found myself sitting at my desk at work and sobbing like a baby. The more I tried to stop crying the harder I would cry. This isn't me. I never show my weakness. I have got to talk to Mommy; she will be able to help me. I made many attempts to reach Mommy by phone. I could not find her. Mommy, where are you when I need you most?

What am I going to do? I cannot drive home in this state. I cannot stay at work like this; I need to get a grip, but I am just not able. I picked up the phone and called the crisis hotline offered by my employer. I made an emergency appointment to see a counselor at 4:30 that afternoon, but I'm not sure that I will be able to wait until then. "I need help right now!"

I was going through my mind searching for someone I might be able to share my feelings with. Someone I would be safe to share my feelings with. There had to be someone in the church I could trust other than my Pastor/Mother. (Did I fail to tell you that my mother is my pastor?) Then it hit me; I could call Elder Pastor, surely he could help me. He had been the pastor of our sister church in Columbus, I had worked with him on several state level committees within the church. He seemed like someone that would listen in confidence, so I made the call.

By the time the call ended, we had prayed, talked and I was laughing. I wanted to cancel my emergency appointment with the counselor but I was afraid that they might think I was suicidal, so I went. (What a complete waste of my time—definitely not worth writing about.)

CHAPTER TWELVE

I was being forced to face my demons. I really was not ready for this but in order to effectively help my daughter, I needed to help myself. I had to face the Beast.

To my surprise finding access to him was easier than I thought it would be. (God always knows what we need when we need it.) The Beast lives in a small city about seventy miles from Cleveland near Sandusky, Ohio, but he happened to be in Cleveland four days a week for therapy on his shoulder due to a work related injury and the facility was between my place of employment and home. I contacted him and explained that I really needed to speak with him, he agreed and we met on the roof of the building where he was receiving care.

The night before and all that day I had butterflies in my stomach along with a bad case of the runs. (I know, WTMI-way too much information.) I was nervous; I did not know how he would react. I did not know what I was going to say. I did not know if I could say anything. You see in my nightmares, I never had a voice, the more I attempted to scream or cry for help the more I realized that there was no sound. I had to do this not so much for me but for my children.

I was still in my second marriage, at the time, and I knew if he ever saw the face of the guy that had damaged me that there would be serious trouble. I informed him of what I was going to do and asked him if he would mind if I had Big Archie drop me off and picked me up. He agreed so I was dropped off on the roof and given an hour to do what I must.

I remember this like it was yesterday. I began by explaining to him why I was there. I had questions. Why? Before he could answer I told him the thoughts in my mind since childhood. I know that we are not *blood* first cousins, perhaps this why you thought it was okay. Maybe, you thought I wanted you to do this. Did I do something to encourage you?

What I heard shocked and comforted me. He said, "Wynette, please don't make excuses for me, there is no excuse for what I did to you, I am sorry." I began to cry not for me for him. For the first time in my life I realized he was hurting inside, I did not know why but I knew he was hurting. (If you don't believe that a victim or survivor -I am a survivor-knows another one when we encounter one, think again.) He went on to say that he knew that he was wrong all along and stated that someone (a friend of his father) had molested him as a child.

I expressed to him that there was no excuse for what he had done to me. I told him how I had become an advocate for children. I watch everything, I see everything, or at least I thought I did. (If you thought I was over protective before…) I asked him if he knew how he had adversely affected my entire life? I was angry, but I was calm. I was direct.

I let him know that I would never trust him but I hoped to one day forgive him. (I have.) I let him know that I was no longer afraid of him, but afraid of what I might do to him if I ever felt threatened by him. I advised him that if we were ever in the same house and if I were in a room alone it would be ill advised to enter that room. I told him that I did not want him anywhere near my children! He was not to hug them, pick them up or touch them in any manner. I really do not know what my reactions would be if he were not to adhere to these requests (okay demands).

His response, again, was beyond my belief. He said, "Wynette, I understand. I know that I can never make up for what I have done to you. I hope that one day you will be able to trust and forgive me. If there is anything I can ever do for you, please do not hesitate to ask."

I reassured him that I was not seeking revenge and that I would never tell his wife. (By the way, my childhood prayer that I never get pregnant by him was answered in more ways than one. The Beast has never fathered a natural child. He is currently in his third marriage, his first two wives did not have children until they remarried and he adopted a child with his current wife.) I left feeling relieved yet sad. I have never again had the reoccurring nightmares where I was unable to cry out—that's right, I got my voice back.

47

Life With A Smile

I must admit I still have some sadness for The Beast. I no longer hate him. I have forgiven him, completely. I know that the forgiveness was more for me than for him. It is my sincere prayer that he finds his peace with God. If God forgives, who am I not to forgive?

I had the strength I needed to deal with LaToya's pain and for that, I am grateful!

CHAPTER THIRTEEN

Is it possible to be independent and interdependent at the same time? I was divorced for the second time. I had stood up to my enemy. I was working and taking great care of my children, yet I yearned for something more.

Big Archie and I started doing family things together. You know, like taking the children to the circus and Disney on Ice. I know that it is not good to play with fire. Archie and I have too much history. Our feelings for one another are too strong. I did not want to want him. I did not want to need him. I knew that I would be heading for trouble.

I fell down on my knees and I cried out to God as never before. These were my words, "Lord Jesus, you know how much I love this man. You know the earnest desires of my heart are to please you. If this is not the man that is meant for me, if it is not in Your will for us to be together, please diminish some of the love I have for him." Now let me warn you, be careful what you ask for, God just might do it.

Big Archie and I have been best friends (male/female) since our days at the insurance company. We would normally talk on the phone daily. (Yes, even during my second marriage.) We would talk about our children. We would ask one another's opinion regarding the opposite sex and we were always honest with one another, even when it hurt. For some strange reason, we did not speak to one another for a two-week period. When he called me at work all he said was "hello" and my response was, "what do you want?!"

I recall thinking, why would you talk to him like that? You have never spoken to him like that. I heard in my mind what could only have been the voice of God saying, "Remember, you asked Me to diminish the love." Whoa, I never felt so reassured in my faith. If God can answer the simplest prayer, just like that, wow! Don't miss understand, I still love that man, just not the same way anymore. I can live not having him romantically in my life and that is only through God.

It was during this time that my telephone conversations with the Elder increased. Elder Pastor showed genuine concern in my well being,

49

emotionally and spiritually. At first he called to check how I was doing after our initial conversation (the day I had my breakdown). After finding out about the first and second break-ins, he called to make sure that we were safe. As I mentioned previously, I was having problems sleeping and he referred me to a scripture to help me. (Proverbs 3:24 - When thou liest down, thou shalt not be afraid: yea, thou shalt lie down, and thy sleep shall be sweet.) I typed this scripture out and taped it to my bedroom wall, whenever I had a problem sleeping I would read it and sleep peacefully. I have given this scripture to many others since that time. Thy sleep shall be sweet! (Thank you, Pastor.)

Elder Pastor and I had many conversations from that point on. I had known him since my childhood. He had been my childhood teacher during our national church convention. I trusted him, which for me is rare. I do not trust very many men. (For any man other than Daddy, Uncle Rob or Uncle Jimmy to earn my trust and respect was a difficult and an almost impossible task.) I was really beginning to enjoy and anticipate my telephone conversations with the man I had only known up to this time as Elder Pastor (really it was by his last name only, but for his privacy I am not mentioning). For the first six months that we talked I only referred to him as Elder (last name).

I was somewhat confused about this relationship, you see Elder Pastor was thirteen and half years my senior. His conversations were friendly (sometimes extremely), yet spiritual. Was I getting my signals crossed? I recall asking my mother, "what does Elder Pastor want?" She stated, "he is from the old school where men like to do the courting. Give it sometime, you'll find out where he stands." He bought me a birthday gift that was really confusing, a beautiful card, but the gift was two Bible study aids, a Bible Dictionary and a commentary, huh? What was he saying?

We had many late night telephone conversations and I knew I was beginning to fall for him. This really scared me. I was not ready for another serious relationship and marriage was out of the question. I had already had two failed marriages and you know what they say, "three strikes and you're out!" Elder Pastor was not even my type. (Alright ladies, we must admit that we all have our preferences whether we state them or not.) I remember early on in our talks mentioning that

50

I had taken care of two husbands and had no intention of ever doing that again. I mentioned that if a man didn't make at least what I made he would have no chance with me. I even told him that I was not interested in a relationship and that I did not have the time or the energy to try to start building a new one. This did not deter him and that intrigued me.

After several months of telephone contact only, Pastor and I had our first official date on October 2nd. (I remember the date because it was the day of my sisters wedding.) We went to the Cleveland Zoo and Rainforest. We walked hand in hand and it was refreshing to find a real gentleman. This was the beginning of a wonderful romance.

Pastor was attentive and caring. He was nurturing and sensitive to my needs. He *noticed* my needs and *attended to them* without my asking. (Boy was this different than my previous relationships—Archie excluded.) I hated to admit it but I was enjoying having him in my life and what was most frightening was that I was beginning to need him. I never allowed myself to need anyone before and especially not a man.

I was driving a very old and ugly Ford Fairmont station wagon that was on its last leg when Pastor asked me to catch the bus to Columbus to visit him. I was a little leery about this, it was December (snowing) for one and what did he really want? But, I decided to go; he had been trustworthy up to this point. To my surprise, when I stepped off the bus, was a brand new Chevy Astro Conversion Van. (He had been listening to our conversations. I had mentioned to him in passing that one day, I would really like to have an Astro Conversion Van.) It was a gift for me. No strings attached. I said no. I cannot accept this. He insisted. He stated, "even if we break up, I want you to have this. You deserve it. If we don't stay together, I will find a way to pay it off sooner. It is yours to keep no matter what." Wow, I must be dreaming someone please pinch me and wake me up. It wasn't a dream. I hopped in and drove my new vehicle back to Cleveland.

A few months later, Pastor asked me to marry him. He told me that I could pick out my own ring but it needed to be at least a one-carrot diamond. I accepted his offer of marriage. (I recalled my conversations with Mommy. I had mentioned that if I ever married

51

again, God would have to show me. I would not be the only one to know and he had better come wrapped in a red ribbon. On our first date, you know the one to the zoo. Pastor came to my door wearing a black suit with a red tie. He was wearing red socks and carrying one red rose.)

Pastor and I had discussed several different possible dates to get married. He came to Cleveland on a weekday, in March, so that we could go apply for our marriage license. In the car on the way to the courthouse, Pastor stated that he needed to tell me something. What could he possibly have to tell me? What he had to say rocked my world, as I knew it. He was married. That's right, he was married. His wife lived in Florida and he lived in Ohio. They had never lived together. He had married her shortly after his divorce from his first wife of seventeen years (the mother of his children). He had mentioned this woman to me in the past, but he said that they had been engaged. He said he knew that it wasn't in God's will for them to be together because he was unable to find work in Florida and she was unwilling to move to Ohio. But married is a far cry from previously engaged.

I was devastated and confused. I insisted that Pastor not contact me anymore and even attempted to give him back the van. He refused to take the van back and ignored my request and continued to pursue me. I must admit I needed him. I asked myself would you rather be miserable without him or miserable with him? (Pay attention to that question.) In May, I gave in to my own needs and continued my relationship with him.

Soon after, I received a letter from the national church headquarters stating that the ADHOC committee was calling me into question with regard to my relationship with the Elder Pastor. His wife had complained to the church and accused us of adultery. (Now, I know that adultery is a physical act, but I guess emotional abandonment was a form of adultery.) I was doing my best not to get angry with this woman. What was she trying to say? Why would she believe this of the Elder? (Hindsight: I later found letters she had written that clarified her way of thinking.) In June, during our national convention, I was placed on probation for a year. I was required not to have any contact with Pastor during this period.

On November 2nd of the same year, Pastor was divorced. We were married on November 24th, Thanksgiving Day. When we returned to our national convention the following year and we were both placed on silence for another year. (Silence requires you to be faithful to all church services, pay all your required offerings but hold no office and have no voice. In other words, you come to church and sit only. You are seen but not heard.) Keep in mind that is a Pentecostal Holiness Church. It's not easy not to clap or sing or stand or shout. All you can do is sit!

I was blind. God have given me away of escape with the probation but I just did not see it. Maybe, I did not want to see it. The first year of my marriage was wonderful. The church part was difficult, but we had each other and that was all that really mattered.

The timing of our marriage was perfect; my employer at the time was laying-off middle management (that was me). I did not have to quit in order to move to Columbus. I took the buy out and it was an enormous buy out for the time (I was to get 80% of my annual salary in one lump sum payment plus a percentage for each year employed, which for me was a little more than eight years and I would still be eligible for unemployment). The catch was we had to work until December 2nd. So for the first two weeks of my marriage, I had to remain in Cleveland. Immediately after work on Friday, December 2nd, my children and I moved to Dublin, Ohio a suburb of Columbus and began our new lives.

CHAPTER FOURTEEN

My new husband and my children were easily spoiled during our first few months of marriage. I was home everyday. The laundry was done. Dinner was ready when they got home. No one had to do chores. They were living high off the hog and I was the hog.

I started working in April of the following year and it seemed that my family had lost their minds. They were of the mindset that I had done it all while I was home, I would continue to do it all. Wrong! Eventually, everyone adjusted and things were running smoothly.

Prior to finding employment, I decided to take my husband on a honeymoon. We never officially had one because of my job in Cleveland. I had to force him to take off work. Not only is he a preacher but he also works for the State. I had received my settlement from my former employer and purchased a cruise to Freeport, The Bahamas.

Pastor was very romantic during this first year of marriage, every month on the 24th he would bring me roses to represent the number of months we were married. The first month it was one red rose, second month two up to our first year anniversary when I received a full dozen of long stem red roses. (What a romantic!)

We returned to our national convention in June and our silence was lifted. In July we found and placed a bid on our dream house. By September we had purchased and moved into our new home. He told me that this home would be my place of refuge. He promised that my children and I would always be safe here and that all of the revolving doors from my childhood would stop here.

In August, during our state convention, Pastor was reappointed as pastor of the Columbus church. Pastor's focus changed overnight from his family to the church. Now, I have been in the church for the majority of my life. I understand that there are responsibilities and concerns that the pastor carries above the other members but I could not understand why it was so difficult, almost impossible, for Pastor to be a pastor and a husband.

Growing up in the church my grandmother was the pastor. After her death in 1988 my mother was appointed as pastor. They were both capable of being wives, mothers and pastors. Maybe, I just needed to give it time. I loved the man I married. I just needed to wait a while. He would come home (at least I hoped so).

Now, I am sure some of you are probably thinking, she was just spoiled rotten and did not want to share the limelight. Well, at first things were a little difficult, but that wasn't it. It was difficult to go from having his complete undivided attention to none at all. No, I am not exaggerating. Everything seemed to be all about the church. Don't get me wrong, I am a firm believer that God should be first in your life but there is a difference between God and the church. God instituted marriage in the Garden of Eden long before he established the church. God is about family first. God should be first, then the family, and then the church.

(I must inject one of my writings here – please bear with me in my folly.)

WHY DID GOD INSTITUTE MARRIAGE?

"And the Lord God said, It is not good that man should be alone; I will make him an help meet for him." (Genesis 2:18) This verse implies that marriage was instituted to meet man's need for companionship. He should not be alone. During creation all living things had been created both male and female, however humanity had only a man, <u>Adam</u> at this point.

God recognized that Adam was alone, not lonely but alone and it was not good. God said he would make him a "help meet". The term "help meet" implies compatibility, someone with whom Adam could relate. (Yes, someone "fit" for him.)

The earth needed population, "be fruitful and multiply"; therefore procreation or reproduction was also a part of God's plan. Family a source of support, encouragement, emotional development and connection, "cleave unto".

Marriage is a union of two separate individuals joining together and becoming one unit. This one unit is intended to work towards one purpose, one goal and for One God.

The joining together (or marriage) also represents God's relationship with His people. He is coming back for His bride. God said He was "married to the backslider". This does not allow us the convenience of living any way we choose; we must maintain a healthy marriage relationship.

Our spiritual marriage should be free from deception, infidelity, distrust and secrets, so should our natural marriages. Healthy marriages require work. God's plan was that we remain faithful to our earthly spouse, just as we must remain faithful to Him.

If you are wondering why I felt compelled to inject this writing here it is because I wanted and want most of all to please God. I worked to keep this marriage viable. I had been divorced twice (and so had Pastor). I felt somewhat justified in my first two divorces because I was (unequally yoked) married to unsaved men. This husband is saved, sanctified and filled with the Baptism of the Holy Ghost. He is a preacher and a pastor this marriage had to work.

But was I *fit for him*? Pastor was well aware of my childhood experiences. I was openly honest with him. I told him things I truly thought I would take to my grave. I trusted in his love. I trusted in his compassion. Most of all, I trusted in his holiness.

CHAPTER FIFTEEN

I had been working now for several months for a chemical company in the Dublin area. I was a customer service representative and my job required some travel. I went from Iowa to Texas to Louisiana and Mississippi. It was fun and exciting but at the same time I missed my family. Being a single parent for so many years (during my second marriage I was still a single parent, partly because my husband wasn't old enough to be a father to my children) made me uncomfortable leaving my children for long periods of time.

Just as the traveling portion of my position slowed, I got ill. I had obtained this position in April and in February of the following year I was hospitalized. I had emergency surgery to have my right ovary, tube and appendix removed. (Why was it emergency surgery? I have a high tolerance for pain and by the time I complained things were serious.)

I returned to work after six weeks, but something just was not right. I kept telling my doctor that I was still having pain. Pain so severe that I felt shooting pains down my legs. It seemed as though he did not believe me. I remember him recording one day after leaving the examination room I was in that I was an enigma (did he think I was making up the pain?). It was not until October when I walked into his office unable to keep anything down and vomiting on his office floor that he decided to hospitalize me and do exploratory surgery. This surgery resulted in my loosing my uterus.

The pain I was having, was not in my head. After examining the uterus it was determined that I had many scars and adhesions on my uterus. The doctors were surprised that I had two children previously based on the damaged done to my uterus.

The counselors were swarming into my room asking if I wanted to talk? If I wanted to explain how this damage might have been possibly done to me? Counselors, social workers, what were they trained for? Couldn't they see that their prying was causing more damage than help? Sure I knew how it happened, but did they really want to hear it? Maybe I should have just shouted it out to the top of my lungs. That big, fat, nasty sloppy, ugly, black cousin of mine ripped me up inside! Maybe that would have shut them up! Instead, I turned my back with tears streaming down my face and calmly said, "No, I don't have anything to talk about."

I healed and returned to work but again it just seemed that something was not right on the inside. I changed doctors; my trust in this doctor just was not there anymore. I had test after test and nothing was found. Eventually, I was diagnosed with IBS (irritable bowel syndrome) and of course there is not much you can do about IBS, you just suffer. I learned to live with it and life went on.

I really felt bad for Pastor, we had been married for just under two years and his wife (me) had gone thru two major surgeries. He had married a wife thirteen and half years his junior and she was sickly. He however (never having been sick above the flu in his life) did not see the severity of my illnesses. In fact, I recall him telling people that I'd had a minor surgical procedure and that I would be just fine. (That should have set off some alarms in my head.)

We continued our normal routines of work, church and family (?).

The children and I wanted a dog. We discussed it with Pastor and he was against it. We had always had pets and we love Chow Chows; we really wanted a dog. By chance, in my travels to Mississippi, one of my customers had a male and female Chow Chow and promised me first pick of the litter when the next litter of puppies came. The sales representative from Louisiana called said he was coming to Dublin for meetings and was bringing me two male Chow Chow puppies (one for my mom and one for me).

I could not tell Pastor, I knew that he would never agree. I knew that if he saw this little ball of fur his heart would melt and it did. Don't get me wrong; we definitely had a heated discussion about my underhandedness. But in the end Bear stayed and we all fell in love with him.

Shortly after returning to work following my second surgery, I received a job offer from a newly developed Managed Care Organization (they handled worker's compensation medical claims). I was most comfortable working in the health care industry so I jumped at the chance. I began my new position as a Customer Service Representative and Trainer.

I loved my new position and I made a friendship that has lasted to this day with Toni. It is ironic that I found friendship in a female named Toni because I am definitely allergic to males with that name. Toni is outspoken and stronger than she realizes. Shortly after our becoming friends Toni was divorced from her husband of twenty years. This devastated her and I was there for her, no matter what. I told her one-day she would be stronger but until that day she could lean on me.

I was really glad as time went on that I allowed her to rely on me because my time was sure to come.

CHAPTER SIXTEEN

I have toiled over how to begin this chapter. I remembered that my daughter's high school counselor gave me a writing assignment so I will start there.

THE DAY MY WORLD CHANGED

Hundreds of thoughts shot through my head. I remember the day she was born: Wednesday, April 1, at 7:26 pm, a perfect little girl; ten fingers, ten toes, a perfectly shaped head covered with beautiful dark brown hair, weighing 6 pounds and 13 ½ ounces. I can still remember her first step and her first word. I remember comforting colds and fighting asthma attacks. I still feel the pain of trying to explain why her daddy was not coming back, after our divorce. I remember holding and rocking her, explaining that we both loved her but we could not live together any more. (How do you tell a three year old that her daddy's not coming back?)

I hear her pleading for a sister or brother and then not wanting that baby in her house. I can still feel the shock I felt when I first noticed pubic hair as she bathed and then the budding breast and a menstrual cycle.

I recall our talks and discussions when we saw teens wanting babies on <u>Sally Jesse</u>; and *how stupid we thought they were.* I remember her first haircut and manicure. I can still see that smile that illuminated her face Christmas morning when she received her first gold ring with her name spelled out at the age of ten and all the gold and diamonds that followed. I can recall, the shock when she returned after a summer with her father, with a second hole in each ear (which I had forbidden).

I yet recall the times they ate (she and her younger brother) and I went hungry, because I could not afford to feed us all. I think of not having a coat that fit or boots in the winter, to ensure that she and her brother had all of their needs and some of their wants.

I remember explaining to her and apologizing for the mistakes I made in my life and praying that she not do the same things.

Please do not misunderstand, I do not regret being a mother, but if I could go back and do it over, I would wait. Married at 18 years old and a mother shortly thereafter, I put off college. Could I work, go to school and be a mother? I willingly gave up college to give my little girl the best start possible. Then five years later, divorced and alone, I find myself pregnant again. Now how could this happen? Where had my religious beliefs gone? What was I doing with my life and how could I take care of two children by myself?!?

Somehow, I did for nine years. It took hard work, tears, struggles, hunger, and emotional and physical exhaustion; but I did it. Then God blessed me, no us, with a wonderful husband and father. He has worked to provide even greater luxuries and care. We have a beautiful home, which we have dedicated to God. So many things that we could only imagine we would someday have, we now enjoy. As I walked through my daughter's bedroom door that Wednesday evening, May 28, and found a boy (young man) undressed in my little girl's bed, all of these thoughts shot through my head.

Some have said, "I know how you must hurt." "I understand what you are going through." "The pain will ease," they said. Then six weeks later, more pain. By telephone, a long distance call, (she was at her grandparents for the summer) my little girl says: "Mommy, I know that you'll be upset and disappointed in me and I'm sorry, I'm pregnant."

PREGNANT, if that word alone did not shatter my heart the events to follow sure would. I slowly discovered that my honest, perfect little girl had not been so honest and perfect, after all. Her boyfriend's family, her little brother and his father, her aunts and friends all knew about the pregnancy before me. She revealed that she had been sneaking the boy into our home for over a year and that she had lost her virginity at 14 years old while spending the summer with her father. (The same summer she had defied me by getting the second set of ear piercing.) Her pediatrician was aware

61

that she was sexually active and she had been careful to protect herself. *How careful – she is pregnant, isn't she?*

Then more thoughts shoot through my head, the times her bedroom door was locked and after entering, her not wanting me to open the closet door to put her clothes away, because "it was a mess." Was the pile of blankets on the floor just blankets or a hiding partner in crime? The small lies: pajama's given to her by the young man's grandmother, were said to have come from the mother of her father's girlfriend. What else was she hiding, how many more lies?

I had the entire summer to get a grip on my emotions, since the children were with my parents. Trust me, I needed the time.

She returned home with stricter rules, distrusting parents and a small bulge in her belly.

The doctor visits began, which required me to sacrifice even more. To juggle my time off work without using up all of my sick or vacation time, I had to take short lunches or no lunch at all.

The anger subsides, but the hurt remains. Then, I hear the heart beat for the first time and see the ultrasound. How can you believe in God and not see the miracle in this? Confusion? To say the least; this just should not be happening to a 16 year old.

The doctor's visits continue and now Lamaze classes. We chose teen Lamaze, so that she would be most comfortable. We went every Monday evening for six weeks from 6:00 to 9:00 pm; a room full of pregnant teens, their mothers and/or boyfriends ranging in age from 14 to 21. Can you imagine, 14?

Educational? Yes, but exhausting. I am wearing myself thin. I go to work, church, doctor appointments, and Lamaze classes. Am I neglecting my son and my husband? Is there enough of me to go around? I continue to make sacrifices and push myself, to do so. I feel the affects, I'm tired, but I cannot sleep. I lay awake night after night. Some nights I cry, some nights I toss and turn, but rarely do I sleep. My migraines have increased in occurrences and strength and I really just do not feel well.

As the time draws near, I worry at night if I will hear her if she goes into labor? Will I be there when she needs me? Am I making the right decisions, even when they are tough decisions? Not just for her, but for me. Allowing her to name this baby, the last name has become a big issue with both families. I strongly feel that a child should have the same name as its mother. I have done it the other way, and I still suffer the cost. When I get prescriptions or buy airline tickets or even apply for insurance and some (unthinking) people ask, "Wow, how many times have you been married?" it still hurts.

I still want to protect her. I still want to hold and rock her. Am I wrong?

We make space for the baby. We try to provide for the needs it will have when it arrives, more costly and timely sacrifices. Am I ready for 3:00 am cries and feedings? Everyone says, "It's her baby, let her do it all!" But she's just a baby, herself. She has to go to school. After all, she is just a junior in high school. She has a promising college future, if she continues to apply herself. Do I let her struggle alone? How could I? Again, I sacrifice!

I do anxiously await his arrival and I know that my love for him will be as great as my love for my own children. But, am I ready? I don't think I will ever be ready. Maybe it's vanity, I don't want to be a grandmother at the ripe old age of 35. I don't want my teenage daughter to be a mother at 16. I don't want her to have to make the sacrifices I have made. I don't want her to be in the position where she may have to choose between school and motherhood, or prom and motherhood, etc.

I know that I cannot change it. I know that I cannot stop it, but I wish that I could somehow put this off until she was older.

I feel as though I am on an emotional roller coaster. I want to be happy and excited and a part of me is. But, that over protective mother is still hurting, still wishing things could be different.

So many people have said to let go of the emotions and let her have it. Let her know how much she has hurt and disappointed you. Share how much inconvenience and pain she has caused. But, she is still my child; my little girl and I must protect her, even from myself.

She once told me, "Mommy, if you were ever to have another baby, I would run away." *Do I get to run away?*

He will be here soon and things will change. I know that God and time will heal these wounds.

He has arrived, February 14 at 4:01 am. He is beautiful, and truly a blessing from God. We will begin from here.

It was Toni that I leaned on as I rode that emotional roller coaster and she held my hand the entire time during the ride. (Thanks Toni, I'll love you forever!)

During her pregnancy LaToya spent one semester of school at home and was home schooled. I expressed to her the importance of maintaining her grades. I informed her that if I had to help her raise her child and support them financially, I would not be able to pay for her college education. I told her that pregnancy does not affect your mind.

LaToya maintained her "A" average while at home and upon her return to school to complete her junior year.

Since LaToya was a minor and our household income was above poverty level she was not eligible for any type of assistance. In order to ensure that our grandson would have medical coverage, Pastor and I had to take legal guardianship of him. Prior to Devon's birth we went to the county courthouse to file for custody of our unborn grandchild.

Devon's father's family helped out a lot in the beginning, but if I remember correctly Devon's father bought diapers twice. LaToya found a part-time job after school at Gap Kids so the majority of his clothing was purchased on her employee discount. Milk and food were my responsibility.

We had one more major concern, childcare. LaToya had to return to school and Pastor and I both worked, who was going to care for the baby? In order to empower my daughter I told her that she would need to find quality care for her baby. I went along with her on all the interviews and we agreed upon in home care with a woman from India, her home was less than a mile from the high school and it would make it convenient for LaToya to pick him up after school.

CHAPTER SEVENTEEN

The childcare interviewing process was grueling. I could not believe some of the things I witnessed during our search. There were homes that cared for children in the basement. (And it looked like a basement.) There were overcrowded daycare centers. There were homes with strict rules for the children and parents, including when it was okay to visit and when it was not. So when we found a home that was clean where we were welcomed in and everything seemed inviting we felt we had made a great choice. The location was pretty perfect, too. Although it was slightly out of my way to work, it was close to school.

We asked all the questions and checked references. So on LaToya's first day back to school, I dropped Devon off. Maybe it was mother's intuition but when I left him that morning something just did not feel right. The care provider met me at the front door took the car seat from my hand and shut the door behind her. I was not invited in, no questions were asked, not even for an emergency number to reach my daughter or me. I had butterflies in my stomach the entire day. I must have called to check on him four to five times. Maybe, I was just being overprotective, I just could not put my finger on it, but something just was not right.

Upon arriving for pick up we were greeted the same way, met at the door with baby in the car seat and the door closed as soon as he was lifted up and the diaper bag retrieved from the care givers hand. I asked my daughter if she was receiving better hospitality. I was not surprised to find that she was being treated the same way I was.

We had six weeks until LaToya would be off for the summer; we had to make some decisions. Devon had reflux; this condition caused him to regurgitate almost everything he ate. We found that with a little barley cereal and very warm milk he would keep things down. The childcare providers method of warming bottles was to run them under the hot or warm tap water. We explained that his milk had to be hot, but she would not follow our request.

Within ten minutes of our arriving home each day, Devon was spitting up everywhere. If you know anything about reflux and infants you know that it is a projectile type (it can shoot six feet or more). We were frustrated, yet at this time we did not have much choice. We certainly did not have time to start the interview process again, so I anointed my grandson with oil and asked God to protect and watch over him and I had butterflies in my stomach for six more weeks.

I had to do something. I decided that I wanted to stay home with my grandson and give him the best care available, his grandmother's care. I discussed it with my husband and we agreed that it might be best and with the cost of childcare, I would be working for childcare and the baby's needs only. I knew that I could not go home without an income. First of all, I am too self sufficient for that. So while I was yet working I had my home certified for in home childcare. I had done my research. I knew the average rate of care for each age group. I knew the state requirements. I passed the fire and health inspections. I had all my forms prepared.

What forms, you might be asking? Don't forget that I am a perfectionist. Remember the childcare provider we had used did not ask for emergency contact information or any other question I felt important for the care of my grandson. I decided to give other children the type of care I had wanted for my grandson.

I had emergency contact forms. I had sign in sheets. I prepared authorization for transportation forms and child profile forms. I wanted as much information possible about the children that would be in my home. I wanted to be well informed and comfortable with every child in my care.

I left my job on July 30th and opened for business on August 10th. I prayed that God would send me children that I would not only care for but that I could truly love. I had seen too many horror stories of child abuse at the hands of caretakers and I was determined that that would never be me. I believe that you cannot harm someone that you love. My first two clients started on August 12th.

Business was a little slow in the beginning but at the end of summer when it was time for school to begin the calls started pouring in. I quickly filled all of my slots and I was content staying home and caring for the children. I was not a baby sitter. I did not sit on babies. I was a professional childcare provider.

We would color and play. We took walks and watched <u>Sesame Street</u>. The older children learned how to spell and write their names. I made up songs that had each child's name in it. That's right each child had his or her own song. For example, my grandson, Devon's song was to the tune of <u>Bingo</u>: God gave him a special name and Devon was his name-o, D-E-V-O-N, D-E-V-O-N, D-E-V-O-N and Devon was his name-o.

One of the parents was pleasantly surprised when she came in one Friday evening for pick-up and with concern said to me, "Ms. Nette, I asked Hannah what she does here and all she ever says is that she plays. This concerns me, do you do anything educational with the children?" My response was children learn through play, have you asked her how to spell her name? "Spell her name? You're kidding me right?" No I'm not kidding what about her colors or shapes? Have you asked her if she can count and how high she can count or does she know her alphabet?

By now this mom was puzzled. "You only play with the children and you expect me to believe she can do all these things." I explained that when we are on the swings and I push them we count. When we take walks and march; we sing our name songs and spell our names. When we wash our hands to insure that we wash for ten seconds or more we sing or say our ABC's.

I had taught Hannah that her name was the same spelled forward or backward. I had told her that it began with Ha and ended with ah and had twin N's in the middle. This tickled Hannah and thus she learned how to spell her name.

Her mother called her over and to her delight three year old Hannah could do all these things and she knew all her shapes and colors.

Needless to say, she never again asked me if I took time out to teach the children.

I had an open door policy. During the hours of operation my front door was always unlocked (to the parents knowledge only). My home had very large window to the left of the front door that gave a clear view into the family room, where the children were during our active indoor times and a sliding glass door on the opposite side of the house. The parents were aware that they could come and visit with their children at anytime during the day. My only request was that if you wake a sleeping child that you comfort or return them to napping state before leaving. It would not be fair to me to wake a comfortably sleeping child and then leave me with them screaming.

I had many children that passed through my home. I was affectionately called Ms. Nette by the parents and children and I loved it. Where else can you get hugs and kisses all daylong and it is not sexual harassment?

I fell in love with my children. They were all my children. There were a few that became a part of my family. I have to tell you about Asha. She was a beautiful baby girl that had suffered a stroke in the womb. Asha was born and diagnosed as having the right side of her brain dead. I remember the initial telephone call and her mother explaining Asha's diagnosis. She was a single parent that had been on bed rest for the majority of her pregnancy and was in danger of loosing her job if she did not return to work within the next week. Asha was almost four weeks old. As much as she did not want to leave her this early, she did not have much choice.

Asha's mother had been searching for childcare for almost two weeks and as soon as she explained her daughter's condition she was either hung up on or told that the provider would need to consider it and would get back to her (which they never did). I was praying as I listened to her pour out her heart. It was if I could hear God say, "You asked me for children you could love!"

Before I knew it I had said. "I would love the opportunity to help you care for your little angel when can we meet?" She came the next morning and I was in love for sure. The sight of this baby did not show the struggles she had endured. The only visible sign was a drawn up left hand. "I told her that I was a minister and asked her if it would be okay if for me to anoint her baby with oil and pray for her?" She cried and said please do. I did and then I instructed her not to fear what the doctors might have said. I told her not to limit what God can do. I told her that Asha was a miracle in process.

She cried and told me the doctors said she might never crawl or walk, that she will probably never speak at least not audible speech. She was told that she would have to care for this child all of her life. Once again, I said, "Do not put limits on what God can do." Asha began her care with me that following Monday. I scheduled her physical and occupational therapy sessions. Her therapist would come to my home. I gave her the prescribed medicines. I bathed her. I exercised her left arm and leg. Most of all I treated her like all the other children.

Devon became her protector. It was if he sensed she needed a little something extra and they became inseparable. She did talk and her first word, contrary to her father's belief, was Devon not Dadda. Asha was the only child in my care other than Devon to call me, "Gran."

When Asha left my care to start school where they could give her additional therapy it literally broke my heart. But I had given her the best start possible. She crawled, she walked (with the aid of leg brace), she ran and boy did she talk. Eventually, her mother got married. I was honored when I was asked to perform the ceremony. My heart broke more when they moved to California.

Anointing Asha became a tradition I carried on to all the children in my care. Many of the parents were unaware that I prayed God's divine protection and care on every child that entered my home.

CHAPTER EIGHTEEN

LaToya completed high school graduating with honors and receiving a full four-year scholarship to The Ohio State University. She was going to receive free housing through a program offered by the college for single parents. She was moving out and taking Devon with her.

The guardianship status was not an issue. I had told LaToya from the beginning that this was done to help her, not hurt her, so I agreed that she should take her son with her. After all I was still his childcare provider and I would see him everyday.

That did not mean I was at ease with this desire to move out. I felt that she could commute to school from home. I tried to accept her need for independence but I was not sure it was for the correct reasons. Below is the letter I wrote LaToya when she had made up her mind to move out:

Dear LaToya:

There are many things that I need to say to you. I have mixed emotions about you moving out. Not because I don't want to let go of my little girl, but I want to know that you are safe.

Safety is more than a secure home and reliable care. I want you to be emotionally safe and whole. I know what it is like to be 18 years old, with feelings and emotions running wild. I know that you want more from your relationship with (her long distance boyfriend at the time). **I can see you setting yourself up for pain.**

Your insistence on moving out and on him visiting are too parallel. (Perhaps, you think I'm blind or stupid.)

You won't see it and you won't believe it, but he is not as serious as you think. You've been burned once and you're setting yourself up to be burned again. If he comes to visit it will be for one thing and one thing only-he'll probably never come back-and he'll talk about you-whether you believe it or not. He's probably already talking about you. When he called last week at 11:40 pm someone else was

on the phone with him. I wonder how often he has people listening in on your conversations.

I don't want you to learn the hard way that you cannot force someone to love you the way you need to be loved. Sex is not love!

Whether you admit it or not I know that sex is on your mind. I also know that you are probably thinking, "Well, if I'm going to be accused of it, I may as well do it." It is an excuse to sin or do wrong.

Just as you see now what I said about naming Devon, one day you'll look back and say, "I should have listened to my mother."

A mother's love isn't always easy to accept. A mother's guidance isn't always the direction you wish to follow. A mother's intuition is not easily understood. But, a mother cannot close her eyes and allow her child to walk into a ditch blindly.

I hope you do what is right. I hope you do what is best for you and Devon.

Love you,

Mom

She moved into her apartment in October and the boyfriend never came to visit. They eventually broke up.

LaToya was doing well in college and was working in the evenings for a large insurance company headquartered in the Columbus area. After her first year she moved to an apartment closer to home and work and everything seemed to be going well with her. She even had a new zeal about her relationship with God.

Shortly after her move LaToya called on the late morning of July 18th to say that she was leaving campus early (she was attending summer quarter to get an advance start on the upcoming year) and was coming by to spend some time with Devon before going to work. It seemed like it was taking her a little longer than usual and I was getting really concerned. You know that mother thing. At the time, LaToya did not have a cellular phone so I had to wait it out. Maybe she made a stop first, I thought. Stop worrying.

My phone rang. I did not recognize the voice on the other end. It was a man with a foreign accent of some sort. He said, "Is your name Wynette?" I said, "yes." He said your daughter was in a bad accident, she is in the car crying and shouting call my mother her name is Wynette her number is 766-____." I was in panic mode, "Where is she? Is she okay? Is someone helping her? Is anyone else hurt?" He replied by telling me the location and saying he did not know the answers to the other questions but that someone had already called 911 and then he hung up.

I frantically began packing up the babies and children. I pulled out the emergency contact cards. I called all the parents and asked that they meet me at the emergency room to pick up their children.

I arrived at the scene of the accident. I felt helpless seeing my baby trapped in that car. The blood was streaming down her face and her eyes were swollen shut. She was screaming in pain as the emergency personnel were attempting to get her out of the car using the Jaws of Life. I was trying to comfort her, but they were pushing me back. I was trying to tell them that I was her mother, but I look so young, they would not believe me.

I was telling her as loudly and as calmly as I could that I was there and that I loved her. I told her to call on the name of Jesus that he would comfort and protect her. And of course, I was doing the same.

All of the parents arrived at the hospital and picked up their children and wanted me to tell LaToya that she was in their prayers. Devon's paternal grandmother arrived. She wanted to see LaToya and she wanted to take Devon in. I stood firm on my decision when I said, "No, he does not need to see his mother like this, she would not want him to see her this way. It will frighten him. Please take him home with you. I have explained to him what has happened. I will call you and update you on her condition.

Life With A Smile

LaToya suffered a major concussion and a broken nose. Initially, they believed that she had broken her pelvic bone. Thank God, the x-rays proved this to be wrong. She has a cut on her left eyelid, only visible when she closes her eyes. She has no memory of the accident, which the police determined to be her fault. She still has occasional headaches and neck pain, but glory be to God my baby is all right.

Because of her concussion, LaToya could not live alone so she had to come home for a few months. I loved the opportunity to once again pamper my child, although I would have preferred it be under more pleasurable circumstances.

CHAPTER NINETEEN

Taking care of LaToya took my mind off my own pain. It had been nearly four years since my last surgery and I was not feeling well, again. I was experiencing severe pain on my left side with shooting pains down my leg. Just as the doctor gave LaToya permission to drive again, I was in need of her help as much as she had needed mine. I had been back and forth to the doctor for about three weeks and now the doctor was on vacation.

I called and explained that my pain was unbearable and the nurse practitioner requested that I come in to see her. Upon examining me she sent me for an immediate vaginal ultrasound. The ultrasound intensified the pain and I know that I heard a heartbeat. How could that be possible? I only had one tube and ovary and my tube was tied. The pain was so great that I never recuperated from that ultrasound. I was now dragging my left leg in order to walk.

My doctor was scheduled to return the following week on Thursday and I was instructed to stay on bed rest. Fortunately, since it was August most of my children were on vacation with their families. I called the doctor's office on Thursday and was told that due to the heavy schedule of the doctor the earliest they would be able to see me was Monday.

I have a very high tolerance for pain but to ask me to wait until Monday; I felt was just plain inconsiderate considering what I had been suffering. I called my mother and told her what the doctor's office had told me. Mommy said, "Nette, you are too calm, they think there is nothing wrong with you. You need to call back and cry. Force yourself to cry if you have to but make them aware in no uncertain terms that you cannot wait until Monday."

It worked. They knew that I had a high tolerance for pain so for me to be crying must have meant that things were bad. I was asked to come into the office immediately and was told that they were going to send me to the pain management clinic to return home with a morphine drip until they could see me Monday.

My doctor, God bless her, saw me walking into her office dragging my leg behind me. If only you could have seen her look of concern. She immediately stopped what she was doing to ask me, "Why I was walking that way?" I explained that the pain had virtually made my leg numb and that I could not move it. She led me to an examination room and checked me over. She said, "You will be having surgery tomorrow morning at 7:00 am. I need you to be here by 5:30 am."

On my way home, I called my husband at work to tell him what the doctor had just told me and his response was, "I'll drop you off on my way to work." I had to have misunderstood him. I just told him I was about to have another emergency surgical procedure and he said he would drop me off on his way to work, what am I his wife or his doormat?

When I got home I immediately called my mother to tell her what Pastor had said. She said, "Don't worry baby, your mommy will be there."

The next morning, you guessed it; he dropped me off on his way to work at about 5:15 am.

Mommy had left Cleveland early that morning to make sure that she would reach me before I went in for surgery. On her way down she called Pastor at work and got his voice mail. Mommy told me that she had left him a voice mail message to say if you were a man and any form of a husband you would be at the hospital with your wife and not at your job.

Mommy arrived at the hospital around 6:15 am and was able to go with me for surgical preparation. Pastor returned to the hospital around 6:45 am.

While preparing me for surgery, I was asked numerous questions. One question about adverse reactions to anesthesia caused me some concerns. I explained that after my previous surgeries I had ran a fever. I did not know if it was related to the surgery or not. The doctors became concerned and wanted to review my medical records prior to performing surgery. So I was not going into surgery at the original scheduled time.

My last surgery was nearly four years prior so my medical records where in storage at an off site warehouse. My doctor explained that she was not going to be able to wait and gave me two options. She would give me something to make me sleep (I had not slept in three days due to the pain) and I could go home and return in the morning or they would keep me if I trusted her to operate at 7:00 pm after caring for her office patients and doing evening rounds. What a choice. Would she be too tired to operate? I knew I did not want to go back home in this much pain so I opted to wait.

The surgical ward was overly crowded that morning. I was relieved to be moved into a corner and whatever they put into my IV and that injection into my rear end did the trick. I started sweating like crazy and before I knew it I was asleep. This routine continued every time I awoke until about an hour before surgery.

Mommy had a meeting to attend in Cincinnati and assured me that she would be back before I went into surgery. Whatever she had said to Pastor must have really made him feel guilty because now he was overbearing. He was hovering like a vulture. He was not trying to console or comfort me. He was just making a point that he was there and his very presence was agitating me.

Mommy returned as promised and I went into surgery that night. I was amazed at how silent the surgical ward was now. It was like a ghost town. The anesthesiologist had done his job and I remember singing in my head, Jesus Be A Fence All Around Me.

I awoke with tubes down my throat and my hands tied down so that I would pull the tubes out (a natural reaction due to the discomfort). Mommy was rubbing my head and saying, "Baby, God was surely with you. You were sicker than you realized." I went back to sleep.

I later learned that when my doctor went in with the scope to see what was going on and to attempt to remove my remaining tube and ovary that she could not see anything. She did not understand what was going on but she later told me that something told her to pull that scope out immediately and cut me open again.

She could not believe her eyes. My intestines were in upside down (remember my complaints about stomach pain – I wasn't crazy). It appeared that after my uterus was removed my intestines were just thrown back in. They were twisted and tangled and they were strangling the ovary and tube, which explained the pain down the leg. If she had not pulled the scope out when she did she would have punctured my bowel and I would have needed a colostomy bag or worse, I could have died.

To my doctors horror was this sight and the knowledge that the surgery department was empty. Had she performed the surgery in the morning there would have been a gastroenterologist available to correct the bowel problem so that she could perform the surgery she had entered me for originally.

There was something she was unaware of; I was singing, "be a fence". She called for help and discovered that a specialist had just completed surgery in the operating room adjacent to the one I was in. He was able to walk right in, scrub in and get to work. The surgery scheduled for forty-five minutes had taken nearly three hours.

The vulture was still hovering and when he was not watching Mommy asked me if I wanted him there. I nodded no and she convinced him that he should go home and get some rest. She also told him that he needed to reassure my children that I was going to be fine. She informed him that as a nurse and mother she could probably help me more at that time and that she would be able to sense when I was awake and give me ice chips (the only thing I could have with the tubes down my mouth and nose). She told him to come back in the morning. He did come back in the morning, laptop in hand and he sat in the corner working on who knows what and watching Bruce Lee DVDs. (Why was he there?)

CHAPTER TWENTY

I know myself better than anyone and I knew that my relationship with Pastor was speeding head first down hill. The very sight of him was beginning to make me physically ill. God forbid he would want to have sex with me. I just wanted to vomit.

My relationship with my husband was quite strained at this point. We were basically going through the motions but I did think that he loved me. I just thought he was having a difficult time expressing it.

A few weeks before our fifth wedding anniversary, I asked Pastor to go with me to a Christian Counselor for marriage counseling. I could see, feel and sense that things were not right and I had never been married five years. I loved him and I wanted this marriage to work. His initial response was adamantly, "No!" He stated that if you have the Holy Ghost you don't need a counselor the Holy Ghost is a counselor. (Well, apparently at this time his or ours wasn't working—at least not in the area of our marriage.)

He did concede to go when I insisted that we needed this. I even stated that at least I needed it. He went and in my opinion he said what he felt the counselor wanted to hear. He would answer the questions posed to him with direct and careful calculation. He would never elaborate or show any sign of emotion. After each session our ride home was filled with tension and his scolding of me for the things I expressed and revealed in the session. After a few failed sessions and his refusal to attend a session alone with our Christian Therapist, I resigned to continue going for personal counseling due to my childhood abuse.

It was obvious that Pastor had a problem with my desire for counseling. I had endured these burdens alone much to long. I needed some relief. Pastor went as far as stating across the pulpit that anyone going to therapy must not have the real Holy Ghost. Now this is where I had to draw the line. I politely stood up and stated to the entire congregation that I was seeing a Christian Therapist and that it was no secret. I boldly expressed that we often tell one another to take our burdens to the Lord and leave them there. I let them know that this was my way of doing so.

It is not always easy to express your innermost feelings with those you have to encounter on a regular basis. I never wanted people to feel sorry for me. I just needed to release some of the pain, guilt and anguish. I never knew who might be listening when I knelt at the altar. God had granted me a way to bring my burdens to Him and that was what I was doing.

I went on to let them (him) know that no one would be able to make me doubt my salvation. If I did not have the Baptism of the Holy Ghost, I would probably be a murderer or a drug addict or a prostitute. By God's grace, I AM SAVED!

For the first time since he was reappointed as pastor over this flock of people one of his parishioners stood up to support me. When Pastor stated, "I don't think that's what I said." This parishioner said, "Oh yes pastor, that was what you said!"

I was totally shocked. You see the majority of the members of the congregation had never supported me in anyway up to this point. In fact they did all within their power to belittle, embarrass and demean me. One of the young men being considered for the Deacon Board approached me after one evening service and told me, "You are not what a first lady should be!" I was willing to take some constructive criticism. I had never been the pastor's wife before, so I asked, "What is it that I am doing or not doing that makes you say this." His reply was, "You are just not it!"

On another occasion, when my husband was away on church business, one of the female deacons came to church fifteen minutes early (this particular deaconess was never on time for church let alone early) just to park in the pastor's parking spot so that I could not park there. I know some of you are thinking that I was just being paranoid, right? Well, that was my initial thought, so I had a conversation with myself and told myself not to get upset. I said a prayer and went into the church. Who do you think was the first person in my face as I entered the sanctuary? She approached me with one of those devilish grins and boldly laughed in my face and said, "I parked in the pastor's parking spot so that you could not. Anyway, the car you are driving is not the pastor's car."

This is just a few of the mean spirited things that were done to me. Whenever I expressed these things to my husband, I was told that I just misunderstood and I should go to the people in love and get clarity. I tried this once with the young man and I knew that I was not going down that road again. Pastor never wanted to believe anything negative about his congregation. I was made to feel like some type of wicked stepmother or I guess step-first lady.

The worst thing was that he believed anything negative that the congregation had to say about me. This was confusing, I was expected to give everyone the benefit of the doubt, but my own husband was not willing to do the same for me. Any thing I said seemed to make things worse. If I stated that I felt a certain way, I was told, "Well, you should not feel that way." (How can you tell someone how to feel?) Whenever there was a hint of an apology it was stated like this: "I am sorry that you feel that way." And he wondered why I was in therapy?

Barb (my counselor) was truly a Godsend. She allowed me to speak as freely as I was able to about my abuse. She helped me to realize that the events of my past were not my fault nor was I somehow branded to be a victim. She allowed me to vent about my marriage and the issues I was facing at the church. She encouraged me and made suggestions on how I might make my situation better. Most of all, she reminded me that I could not change others. I had a choice, change myself, accept others as they were or stop trying to please people whom I obviously would never be able to please. I chose the latter.

Barb also helped me to understand that predators search out their victims. She enlightened me to a study where a sexual predator was placed behind a one-way glass and allowed to observe a classroom and then asked what if any student he would choose to victimize? Surprisingly, the children he picked out had previously been victimized. They were survivors of physical abuse, sexual abuse or had witnessed some type of violence in their lives. (So it wasn't me, it was them; they were the sick ones!)

Life With A Smile

Barb had been trying for months to get me into the sand room. This was a room full of toys and figurines and all types of items that you could use to tell your story in the sand. I was struggling with opening up to Barb. I would hint or touch around the issues but I did not think I would ever be able to fully express my pain. Barb was okay with this she just wanted me to get better. She told me that there are many people who wanted to remember the tragic events of their childhood. She told me that she wished just for a moment they could meet me, someone who wanted to forget the past and the pain.

I am a firm believer if your mind is protecting you from memories of the past, be thankful. I honestly wish that I did not remember. I finally agreed to go into the sand room. I was reluctant at first. This seemed like a place for children and I cared for children day in and day out, I was not interested in playing.

It seemed without thinking I began to build my world in the sand. I had a home protected by a fence and a lion. (The lion took the place of my Chow. She didn't have a Chow. Since a Chow looks like a lion in the face and a bear from behind I choose a lion.) I had a guardian angel on the roof and another guardian angel holding the children (this was me the child advocate vowing to protect the innocent). And then there was King Kong, towering over the house and the angels just waiting to destroy the safety of this home. I stood in silence. I looked at the scene I created. I began to cry silently and out of nowhere, I just reached up and knocked King Kong down. I hit him so hard he fell off the sand table and landed somewhere across the room. I think this took Barb by surprise as well. I never went back to the sand room. I never needed to.

It seemed that day I decided that I was not going to be a victim anymore. I was and I am a survivor! I had finally fully regained my strength. My eyes were opening to a lot of things. It was time for change.

CHAPTER TWENTY-ONE

I began to see Pastor for who he really is. He is a predator. He is a different type of predator, but a predator just the same. He preys on the weak.

Pastor needs to be needed. You see our relationship began when I was in need. I was in need of emotional support. I needed someone to show me unconditional love. I needed someone to understand me. Pastor seemed to be able to fulfill these needs.

The problem was that I bounced back. When I was able to stand on my own two feet emotionally; he did not have a place in which to prey upon me. As I look back, I realize that my strength began to return at about the same time he was reappointed as pastor of the church.

So his neglect had as much to do with me as it did with him. He felt as though I no longer needed him. I did not need a leaning post, but I did want and need my husband. I guess I just was not needy enough.

The problems in my marriage affected my children. My daughter once asked, "Mommy, do I need to make an appointment to talk with Dad?" She continued, "I told him a week ago that I really needed his help with something important and he has not taken the time to speak with me yet."

When I married Pastor, I was under the impression that I would finally have some help with parenting. I was sadly mistaken. Whenever the children asked him anything he would always refer them back to me. "You need to ask your mother," he would say.

Pastor was excellent at manipulating the truth or painting a picture that would cloud your judgment. I was beginning to realize that the things he shared with me about his first wife and children were his twist on the events. His relationship with his sons was strained and I now understand better why. If he was not capable of being a husband, how could I expect him to be a father? More so, if he was not a father to his biological children, why did I think he could be a father to my children?

Pastor admitted that he was jealous of my son's relationship with his father. When my son was the lead in a play in the sixth grade, Pastor was offended that my son's father and grandfather (the Archies) drove down from Cleveland to attend on opening night. His exact words were, "In the future, I will just stay home and you all can support your son." I attempted to help him understand that my children have always had a great bond with Big Archie and that would never change, however he was also their Dad and had a right to be there. Little Archie would not have understood if Pastor had not been in attendance.

Pastor's relationship with LaToya has always been a little better than his relationship with Archie. Maybe this was because he never had and always wanted a daughter. His relationship with my son became increasingly strained. It seemed as though he never had a kind word for my son. He was critical and sometimes cruel in his manner of speech. I knew that I had to do something.

I had consciously made a decision to try to work on making this marriage viable, but my son did not have to suffer for my decision. I thought about it for months, but could not bring myself to act on my thoughts. My son was coming home from school and going straight to his room. He would not come out accept to use the bathroom or eat. I found out later that when everyone else went to bed, he would come out to the family room to watch television or venture to the basement to get on to the Internet and of course that spelled trouble.

I made the hardest decision of my life. With tears in my eyes I called Big Archie. I started the conversation by saying, "Archie, I have considered this for sometime now but could not bring myself to this point. Please don't interrupt me because if I don't say it now, I will never say it. I want to know if you would like Little Archie to come and live with you? I want to make it clear that I am not sending my son away. I want you to know that this is the last thing I want to do, but my son is suffering, he needs his father, he needs you."

Archie's response was, "I would be honored to have the opportunity." He went on to tell me how much of a wonderful mother I was and how I had given him such a great foundation. I was shaking and crying. I could not believe what I had just said. I went on to let Big Archie know that there would be some conditions: Little Archie had to attend church in Cleveland. I did not want him exposed to certain things. He agreed to all my terms. I told him that I was just in the thinking stages and I would get back to him. I also told him that I had not shared my thoughts with our son at this time and to please not mention it.

My next step was to share my thoughts with my husband. I wanted him to be aware of my concerns and my reasoning. His response was, "I can't help you make that decision!" My thought was then why are you here?

I turned to the one I knew could help me, Jesus. I prayed and fasted for three days and nights and then I called Big Archie again to let him know that I wanted Archie to complete the eight grade and stay the summer at home (he had always spent the summers with his father). Archie was to begin high school in Cleveland.

Then I had to discuss this with my son. He was excited about the opportunity but he was a little scared to show his excitement for fear that he would hurt my feelings. He said, "Mommy I don't want to leave you here by yourself. LaToya doesn't live here, I'll be in Cleveland; will you be alright?" I knew what he was really thinking, how can you stay in this house with this man?

I reassured my son that I was not offended by his excitement and that I would be just fine. I informed him that I would still have a very active part in his parenting. I let him know that if he needed me for anything I would be there. Most of all, I wanted him to know that I was not giving him away or getting rid of him. I wanted him to know that my heart ached and that I was screaming inside, but I had to do what was best for him.

Big Archie immediately began making preparations. He spoke to his parents about Little Archie living at their home because of the better school system in the suburbs. He was checking out the sports programs. (Little Archie had wanted to try out for football and basketball in Dublin, but with my running the daycare and Pastor's refusal to transport him to practices and tryouts it never worked out.)

We went through the court systems to make Big Archie the residential parent and everything was set in order, at the end of the summer my fourteen-year-old son would be leaving his mother. It was the ultimate sacrifice. I was conflicted and I was hurting, but had to do what was best for my son, no matter how much my heart ached.

Ironically, the day I came home from the hospital, after having my last ovary removed and my bowels reconstructed, was also the day that my son left home. I was truly a basket case. I really wanted to blame my husband and part of me hated him for this. For me, I was betraying my son and myself. The very thing I despised Jean for the most, giving me away, is what I was doing to my son. I love this boy more than my own life. I was not giving him away. I was doing what was best for him. I cried silently as they drove away but that night I had a good let it all out cry.

Imagine my horror when I received a telephone call from the emergency room on my birthday. The caller said, "Your son is in the emergency room and we need some information." My response was, "I'm not answering any questions until I know if my son is alright!" She immediately said, "I apologize, how inconsiderate you must think I am, your son is okay, we think he broke his wrist in his first football practice."

Archie healed and my heart mended, but it broke over and over again each time I saw him or he came home for the holidays or summer vacation and I had to send him back. I felt all those feelings of betrayal and sadness each time.

CHAPTER TWENTY-TWO

I was beginning to tire of the daycare and had considered closing it and finding employment. I discussed it with my daughter and my husband and they both agreed that I should do whatever I felt was best for me. Devon was a very active, healthy and intelligent three-year-old and he would surely be able to tell us if anything leery was going on in a daycare.

My sister, Celeste called from Harrisburg, Pennsylvania to tell me that she really needed to move away and would like to come to Columbus. She was certain that she would be bringing her two young daughters but was uncertain of her youngest son (he would be turning seventeen and did not want to move with her). We had several telephone conversations between February and May. She had made up her mind that she would be moving to Columbus on Memorial Day. She convinced me that she would help me with the daycare and that I should probably keep it open. She also told me that if I wanted to venture out and find a part-time job for some adult interaction, she would be willing to cover the daycare.

We began preparing our rental property, which had been vacant for nearly two years. We wanted it to be perfect for Celeste and the girls. The house was right next door to the church so we knew that we would be able to check in on them and assist them in any way possible. There was one problem we were unaware of, black mold.

Celeste is bi-polar, so when I arrived in Harrisburg with a U-haul in tow to pick her and the children up, she was sitting in the middle of the floor with stacks of items to be packed but nothing packed. She had told me that she did not have many boxes so I had also brought boxes with me. Celeste was at a low so she was unable to help me pack her things. I packed her entire house in two days and on Monday morning we were loaded and ready for our trip to Columbus.

Upon arriving we ended up unloading her furniture into the dining hall of the church because the renovators were not quite finished. They had not put down the carpet and they were still working on the kitchen floor. Two weeks later we moved everything into the house.

Celeste and the girls never spent even one night in that house due to the black mold. For one, Celeste has asthma and was adversely allergic. Secondly, I would not have left her there. We did not know if the mold was the type that would make you ill and I wasn't willing to take that chance. So, Celeste and the girls came home with me. They all slept in my son's bedroom. To this day, I don't know how they did it for little more than a year, three of them in one bedroom.

My home had three bedrooms. LaToya's bedroom had been converted to the sleep room for the daycare children. Archie was in Cleveland and we had never changed his room because he was home for the summers and for the holiday breaks. And there was the master bedroom, but that was Pastor's room.

Everyone settled in and things were going well. Unlike me, Celeste likes to cook. Pastor loved having dinner everyday, again. The daycare parents and children fell in love with "Ms. Celeste" and I decided to keep the daycare doors open.

Business was good with daycare and with Celeste's assistance we were able to take in a few more children.

In October, I started feeling ill again. Now what could it possibly be? I was sick and tired of being sick and tired. I was not able to eat anything and anything I did eat did not stay in. I was having severe pain on my right side and it even hurt to breathe at times. I was diagnosed with gallstones and I was going to need my gallbladder removed. Fortunately for me, I had my sister this time.

The attention and care Celeste gave me must have made Pastor feel guilty. Perhaps, he remembered his conversation with my mother from my surgery a year or more earlier, because he had no problem staying at the hospital and taking me back and forth for testing this time.

My gallbladder was surgically removed and I now have no other organs that I can live without. (So for any physician or surgeons reading this, please find another pincushion, I have nothing left to give.) Celeste nursed me back to health next to mommies; sisters do well.

I was beginning to heal nicely, so for the Thanksgiving holiday Celeste decided to take the girls and go back to Pennsylvania for a visit. I received a telephone call from a woman needing care for her infant twins (boy and girl). She expressed that she needed immediate care because of her then current provider being accused of child abuse. A family member was watching the babies that day but she needed to interview and find care right away. It was the Wednesday before Thanksgiving and I was closing for the Holiday weekend and not reopening until Monday. She wanted to interview on Friday and I explained that not only was it the Holiday but also my wedding anniversary and I would not be able to interview however I was willing to interview that evening and miss my regular church night service if they could come right away.

They arrived with the two children and we mutually decided that they would begin care the following Monday. My rates were beyond their budget and I knew what it was like to struggle so against my better judgment I gave them a discounted rate. I remember the mother saying, "You don't get a pay raise when you find out you are having twins. We were not financially prepared for two babies." I wanted to help them.

When they arrived the following Monday; they came carrying baby water and all kinds of items that I did not need. I explained that I have water delivered for the daycare and that they might be able to save a little money by not bringing water to me. They would only need the water for home.

It was easy to fall in love with these angels. Noticeably there was something distinctly wrong with the male baby. His head seemed a little larger than normal. I was concerned about his development and shared some of my concerns with his mother. She seemed unconcerned except that he was clumsy and beginning to crawl so she wanted me to keep the gym mats in the family room at all times because he was always falling over. After a few days of him falling off the edge of the mat (it was only about three inches thick) I decided he would probably hurt himself worse by falling off the mats so I only used them when we were sitting on the floor and playing or exercising with the babies. I decided not to be overly concerned and cared for him as I did all the other children.

Then there was a concern about diaper wipes. I required all of the parents to supply wipes for their children. The wipes were used for diapering and clean up after eating. The twins' mother told me that she could not afford to buy the wipes. So I bought them.

There seemed to be a lot of things she could not afford. It was the dead of winter and the male child was not wearing undershirts. She explained that he had out grown all of his undershirts and it was not in her budget to buy more, so I bought undershirts. (I told you that I considered all the children as my children.) Now, what they could afford was to go to Florida and Disney World for the last week of December through the first week of January and they did not want to pay me before leaving. (In business be men.) My contract clearly stated that I am paid in advance for care and that there was a holding fee for time away from care. (I should have known then that I was headed for trouble with this family.)

The girl twin and both parents came down with a stomach virus prior to their departure. And the boy twin was ill during their trip. They returned to care on Monday, January 7th.

I had sprained my ankle the proceeding Saturday and I was on crutches. Celeste had once again gone to Pennsylvania for the Holiday Break and had not made it back home yet due to a winter storm. So it was Monday, I was on crutches with a house full of babies.

I had prepared the house prior to the arrival of the children to make everything easily accessible and even brought a stroller in the house so that I could transport the children to the sleep room. (I should have followed my first mind, to call my next door neighbor over for back-up; but no, superwoman thought she could do it all on her own.)

I had fed all the babies and they were napping with the exception of three: the twins and another infant. I was diapering the one infant in my lap with my leg propped by the ottoman to the rocker, when the something happened that would change the course of my life. The male twin who had been pretty miserable that day, (his mother thought maybe he had not fully recovered from the virus), crawled over to his sister and attempted to snatch a toy from her. The female twin was unable to crawl and was lying on her belly playing quietly but let out a yell when her brother tried to take her keys (the large plastic ones with knobs and stuff). I immediately told him to not to take his sister's toy and leaned over to give him another toy. He went from the crawling position to a sitting position so I refocused my attention to the diapering (it was a messy diaper), when I heard a squeal and before I could react it had happened.

The baby girl had suddenly released her grip on the keys and with his greater pull from the sitting position; they slapped him in his face. I immediately laid the baby I was holding down on the floor and picked up the boy baby to comfort him and to try to take a look at his face. There did not seem to be much damage from the first look so as he quieted I completed dressing the baby I had been diapering and placed her in an exer-saucer. I hopped into the kitchen and prepared a first aid ice compression for the injured child. He did not like the ice compression at all so I had to use some pressure. As I rocked him in the rocker and applied the ice he began to quiet and was falling asleep.

As I was rocking him, I telephoned his mother at work to tell her what had occurred and to obtain permission to give him some infant pain reliever. He let out one more yell as I was speaking to her and she agreed that I should give him the medication. I described to her the light bruising that I saw and expressed that she might want to come get him early to have him examined by her pediatrician. I was concerned about the bruising close to his eye. The incident had occurred close to 1:00 pm and I telephoned her at or around 1:45 pm. Ironically, the parents did not arrive to pick up the children until after 5:30 pm.

The baby had napped from about 2:30 until 5:00 pm and when he awoke I saw more bruising. I was sincerely concerned. When the parents arrived I was icing his injuries and once again encouraged them to seek medical attention for the baby and they assured me that they would.

The next morning the father called to say that they were going to keep the babies at home that day to care for the injuries. I inquired as to the well being of the baby and he told me that he would be okay but they were concerned about my explanation of the injuries. I assured him that things occurred as I had explained and told him that the parent copy of the injury report was available for him.

The father called back about an hour later and stated that he was coming to get the incident report and to pickup the children's things and they would not be returning to care. When he arrived he was pleasant, I gave him all of the items that belonged to the twins and the incident report. As he was leaving, he stated that he was sorry that things occurred the way they had and once again made mention of his concerns for his son's well being. Then he turned to my sister, Celeste and said, "If you need my help moving the remaining items of your furniture into storage don't hesitate to call me." With that he left.

Two days later a detective knocked on my door. He explained that he just wanted my version of the events. I gave him a copy of the incident report and the toy keys. I had taken the keys from the box of accessible toys and had intended to throw them away. (In the past if a child was injured by a toy, I normally removed it to ensure that no one else would be hurt in the same manner, whether a scratch or something more.) The detective left me his card and told me at my convenience (due to my ankle sprain) that he would like for me to come to the police headquarters' to repeat what I had told him officially.

I called the next day to let the detective know that I would like to come in as soon as possible and was willing to come that day. (I had nothing to hide and nothing different to tell so I saw no need to put off going to the station. I had also spoken with my brother/friend, you know the peace officer, and was assured I had nothing to be concerned about, just to tell the truth.) The detective told me he could not see me that day but set an appointment for the following day.

When I arrived at Dublin Police Headquarters I was greeted warmly and led to a small room where I was left alone for approximately ten to fifteen minutes. The detective returned with a notebook and again asked me to state the events of the previous Monday when the baby was injured. I again told him the events. He asked if I had anything more to add and I stated no. He excused himself from the room and said he would be right back.

When he returned he was carrying an envelope. He sat down at the table and told me that I was a liar. He did not believe anything that I said. He told me that I had beat the baby and shaken him. Then to my horror he pulled out pictures of the baby boy that shocked me. There were additional bruises and injuries that were not on the child when he left my home. (I had not taken pictures because I had used all my film over the Holiday and due to my injury had not had an opportunity to get more film.) I wanted to cry, not for me, for that child. I believe I felt a tear drop.

The detective kept badgering me. He told me that he could have arrested me the day that he came to my home but he knew that I was a good person, based on the other people he had spoken to about me. (Of course, he had never spoken to anyone.) He insisted that I admit that I hurt this child. I told him, "You will not make me say that I did something that I did not do!" He told me that he could prove that my fingerprints were on the child's face. I told him they probably were that I had been turning his face to apply ice, but I was certain that I had not applied enough force to leave the handprint I was looking at. Then I told him that if I felt that I had done anything wrong I would not have willingly come to the police station without consulting an attorney.

With that he let me leave, but informed me that the investigation was not complete and that he was turning things over to children services. I could not believe what was happening. When I returned home, my sister informed me that children services had already been to my home and that they would be returning in a day or so. My head was spinning. I did not know what to do next. I called the attorney that had assisted me with my daughter's custody issue and he referred me to another attorney due to the nature of the case.

I consulted with the attorney and paid a $1,500 retainer. My next step was to inform the other parents. This was one of the hardest things I had to do since the opening of the childcare. I was taking a chance on losing all of my children and my income. To my surprise the parents rallied to my support. Not one of them pulled out of care because of this incident. They began writing letters of reference and character. They wanted to help. From January to March, I heard nothing further from the court systems.

CHAPTER TWENTY-THREE

Things with my marriage were not improving and Celeste thought she was causing adverse affects in my relationship. I tried to reassure her that things were bad before she arrived and she had nothing to do with the strain on my marriage.

Pastor was back to his routine of coming home saying "hello" and going straight to his bedroom and closing the door. We were made to feel like intruders if we knocked or entered for any reason. We would ask him if he wanted to join us for dinner or if he wanted his plate in his room. Some days he came out but most days he did not.

I hated entering that room. I did not want to sleep in there. I did not want him to touch me. I did not want to be his wife in the bedroom when I was not treated like his wife in any other aspect of our living. I was his wife in name only. I felt like a showpiece. I do not do well with show and tell.

I had reached my limit in my relationship or lack there of with Pastor, so I moved out of his bedroom to the living room couch. I slept on the couch for a week without one question or search for me from my husband. After a week my back could no longer handle the couch so I rearranged the daycare sleep room and brought up the futon from the basement. This room became my bedroom at night and the children's sleep room during the day. It wasn't until I moved my clothing from the master bedroom closet that he decided to inquire as to what was going on. I politely told him that I could no longer coexist in his room. I needed to have space where I did not feel like I was in the way or a bother; so, I moved to the bedroom at the other end of the house.

We had been married now for a little more than seven years. Celeste witnessed some of the mistreatment from the church congregation and this angered her. It saddened me that she was exposed to these struggles because Celeste was not saved. It is nearly impossible to win someone over to the Lord's side if those confessing to be saved act unseemly.

Life With A Smile

There were a few people in the church that Pastor had carefully instructed me to steer clear of. (Remember, I said he was good at manipulation.) He had convinced me that they were troublemakers and that if I befriended them I would soon find out on my own that I had made a grave mistake. Mysteriously, these people that he adamantly requested that I avoid were the very ones that came to my aid when I was being mistreated or when I was ill.

My grandson's godparents were two such people. Goddie and Deac were constant in their love and devotion. It was Goddie that cooked and brought my family and me dinner when I was recuperating after surgery. It was Goddie that came to run the vacuum or make my bed. (Where were the so-called good Christians?) It was Deac that helped out financially when my daughter had to fight a court battle threatening the custody of her son. (By the way, Pastor stated he could not afford to fight nor did he feel that it was his battle. Some how he had forgotten that he and I were the legal guardians of this child.)

Then there was Wanda. Wanda and I had been childhood friends but time and circumstances had separated us. We were not enemies we just had not had the opportunity to rekindle our friendship. For some strange reason my husband did everything within his power to maintain a wedge between us. Any thing worth having is worth fighting for and the more he insisted that I stay clear of her, the more I wanted to spend time with her.

Everything I knew about Wanda was good. She was married with two little girls. She was a pastor of a mission in an eastern suburb of Columbus. She worked everyday; so what was so wrong with her? We began spending time together shopping and have lunch or dinner on the weekend with her girls. We reminisced about our childhood friendship and we were really enjoying rekindling it on an adult level.

In order to eliminate some of the conflict with the parishioners and having to deal with my husband, I began attending service at the mission. The bond between Wanda and I strengthened and I was glad to have someone close that could relate to me on both the carnal and spiritual levels.

96

In March, I received a letter from children services stating that the investigation found me responsible for the injuries to the child and they were submitting their findings to the county prosecutor. I called my attorney and he assured me he would investigate. Again everything was quiet.

My daughter was pregnant again and expecting a girl in April. With all of the confusion I was facing and the fact that I knew I would not be able to remain in my farce of a marriage, I went to court and gave my daughter back custody of her son, my grandson, on her twenty-first birthday. Three days later my daughter gave birth to a beautiful baby girl and of course I was there to witness her birth. I shall forever know her as my "Nya-Love".

It was painful to think that I would not be able to bond with this baby the way I had with my grandson, but I knew I would love her just as much.

June as you might remember is the month of National Convention of the church and I was preparing to attend. Right before leaving, I again phoned my attorney to find out what if anything was going on with my case. He informed me that nothing was going on that he had been checking continuously and found nothing. A day later I received a letter in the mail stating that I had been indicted by the grand jury in May. I was furious with my attorney. What was I paying him for?

I telephoned the referring attorney and told him what had occurred and that I was also in need of a good divorce attorney and he gave me the name of another attorney. I called the inactive attorney and requested a refund of my retainer based on the knowledge I had obtained and his lack of attention to my case. Then I called "Mad Dog".

My attorney affectionately referred to as, "Mad Dog" by his grateful clients and his not so grateful opponents was a Godsend. He agreed to take both my cases and initially accepted $500 as a retainer.

I left for the convention waiting for God's deliverance both spiritually and legally. I had taken the correspondences courses and on the final Thursday of the convention was awarded Top Scholar or Valedictorian of the class. I was humbled and honored. I could not believe that my work exceeded that of elders, evangelists, other ministers and deacons. I humbly requested the prayers of the church that God might find me worthy of his gifts.

My cellular telephone rang later that night. It was my sister, Celeste and by the sound of her voice I could tell that she was considerably shaken. She began to tell me that the police had surrounded my home looking for me. Celeste and I resemble one another and they made her prove that she was not me. She informed the police that I was out of the state at the church convention. They had given her a card and a telephone number for me to call immediately.

How could this be? I was just awarded Top Scholar in the church and the police were looking to arrest me. I called Mad Dog informed him of the events and gave him the phone number. He called me later to tell me that he had spoken with the police and they assured him I would not be arrested upon my return so he told me to come home as planned the following day.

Mad Dog called me about midnight Friday. I was home. He informed me that we would be going to court Monday morning that he would request that I be allowed to return home. His exact words were, "Relax Wynette, you are not going to jail." I called my parents and they agreed to come down and go to court with me.

Monday morning I did as I was instructed. I did not have time to eat breakfast and it wasn't a major concern, I just wanted to get to court and get this over with; then, I would have a sit down meal with my parents and Pastor.

To Mad Dog's surprise and my horror, the judge never allowed me in the courtroom. He stated that I had to be processed and that I had to be arrested. As Mad Dog came to explain this to me, two police officers one male and one female approached me and placed me in handcuffs. I was shaking uncontrollably. I had never been in trouble in my life. My worst offense in life was speeding. What was happening to me?

As I was being led away, Mad Dog was shouting, "Don't worry I'll get you out of here, but if I can't get you out today, you will be here until Wednesday!"

Wednesday? They must be joking!

CHAPTER TWENTY-FOUR

What a turn of events, four days ago I was being honored in the church as the National Top Scholar and now I am being led away in handcuffs and about to be stripped searched. I was shaking like a leaf, partly because of shock and fear and partly due to the fact that I had taken my medicine and had not eaten. The tears were in full flow but I was silent.

I had to remove my ponytail holder and all bobby pins from my hair. My bra was an under wire type so that was taken away and my panties were not white so I was not allowed to have them either. I learned quickly that I was only permitted to wear white and that I had to do exactly what I was told.

Having to squat and allow someone to examine every crevice of my body was like reliving the molestation and rapes of my youth. As the tears streamed down, the female guard asked me as kindly as possible, if she had done something wrong. I shook my head to indicate no, as I cried even harder she asked again. I mustarded enough strength to say, "You are only doing your job."

If you are not claustrophobic, you will not understand the next horror I faced. I was taken to a cell that was L shaped and about five feet wide and 8 feet long including the L. Another woman was in there asleep on the concrete bench. I was screaming and in a state of panic internally, but I uttered no words, my only expression of what I was feeling was tears.

It seemed that once again, I had lost my voice. I heard my name called and I was taken from the cell to a desk in the center of the main area and asked to identify my belongings and sign a paper acknowledging the same. I was taken back to the cell for what seemed like hours. My body was now jittery from lack of food and water. Once again the door opened and my name was called. The voice asked, "Have you been fingerprinted?" I answered, "No." The voice then asked harshly, "Why weren't you fingerprinted when you were arrested by the Dublin Police Department?" I responded, "I was never arrested by the Dublin Police Department, sir, I was brought here from court."

I was lead away to another room where my handcuffs were removed and I was photographed and fingerprinted. Now I better understand why the mug shots of criminals that are shown on television look so bad. After having all the items removed from your hair placed in prison scrubs and left to sit for hours it seems reasonable that one would not look their best.

The person taking the photos and doing the fingerprinting kept telling me to stop shaking, but never asked why I was shaking so badly and I never opened my mouth except to reply to direct questions I was asked. I was taken back to the cell for what seemed like a few more hours. I tried to sleep to get rid of the shakes but sleep escaped me, so I sat with my feet on the concrete bench, knees pulled to my chest and my back against the hard cold cement wall in complete and utter silence.

A few more women were placed in the cell and then the doors opened and we were all lead to another side of the building where there were the caged type cells. There was one big area approximately fourteen by fourteen with about six to eight individual cells to the right of the larger room. Out side of the large community area of the cell was a television just far enough out of reach that we had to watch whatever was on. Once again the handcuffs were removed and I was issued a thin mat the kind children use in a day care center but much more beat up and as hard as a brick. The sheet issued was worse. It was supposed to be white but I cannot even say that it was gray. It was gross and it was ripped and raggedy. I am and have always been a neat and clean freak and the very thought of germs make me physically ill. This was going to be the death of me. Mad Dog had to be working to get me out of here.

I soon realized that my estimation of time was not that far off because we were being served dinner. I was grateful to be given anything to eat. I was famished. Surprisingly, the food smelled great and my stomach was growling very loudly. I could smell that it was fried chicken but I could not determine the other smells. I waited my turn and took my tray to the picnic type table and sat down to eat. The tears were still streaming uncontrollably. I could not stop crying no matter how hard I tried.

My excitement about having something to eat turned as soon as I uncovered my meal. It was fried chicken all right but the skin was burnt and wet. I had no idea what it was wet from because the green beans were bone dry. The roll was also wet and uneatable. I was hungry so I decided to remove the burnt wet skin from the chicken and just eat the meat, think again. The inside of the chicken was dripping with blood; it was not done. How they were able to burn the outside and the inside be raw was beyond me, so I forced myself to eat the green beans and drink the milk. It was just enough to take away the shakes.

Not soon after the trays were removed the guards reappeared and we were ordered to form a straight line bringing our mats with us. Once again I was handcuffed but this time I was joined to two other women and our legs were also shackled together. We were led to an elevator and then to a van (the kind with a barred gate separating the passengers from the driver) and were told that we were being taken to the workhouse.

What exactly is a workhouse? What type of work was I going to have to do? Boy was I naïve. (You see other than divorce, a traffic ticket and the issues with my daughter, I had never been to court before and of course I had never been arrested.) It was called the workhouse, but you did not go to work, you just went to be locked up in large cellblock with a lot of other women awaiting trial or serving out their short-term sentences.

Upon arrival, I was once again frisked. The words "spread them" makes the hairs on the back of my neck standup to this day. I closed my eyes and prayed, "I am yours Lord, and You said touch not my anointed and do my prophet no harm." And the tears that had momentarily stopped were once again in flowing freely.

Then came the medical examination. A guard with gloves checked the head of every inmate for lice, asked if you were wearing false teeth and if you take any type of prescription medicines. When this was completed we were issued our prison packets, which consisted of a toothbrush, a sample tube of toothpaste, a cup, a spoon, washcloth and towel, a pillowcase and sheet (worse then the ones from the courthouse cells) and a mat. All of the items less the mat were placed in a brown paper bag to make it easier for us to carry. Then we were told that if we did not have all the items less the toothbrush and toothpaste when time came for us to be released, we would not be released. To my horror, I later realized that I was not issued a towel only a washcloth, one I was sure I would never use.

We were lead down several hallways and lined up against wall after wall as each set of inmates were lead to their respective cellblocks dragging our mats and other issued belongings with us. This was not an easy task wearing those over sized plastic flip-flops we were issued.

When I reached the cellblock to which I was to be assigned and the door opened I could not believe my eyes. In my worst dream, I would have never imagined this! The room had three rolls of metal bunk beds with four beds in each roll. The room was designed to sleep twenty-four women but with me and the other women that entered with me there were at least thirty women. I was still silent and still crying as I entered and looked for a place to rest the load I was carrying. One of the ladies pointed me to a top bunk in the middle row recently vacated by a lady that had just been moved to the women's prison in Marysville. How I was going to get my old behind up there was beyond me, but it was better than the floor and I would definitely feel safer than being on a lower bunk. I had heard the horror stories about being in jail and I was certainly not willing to endure more hardship at this point.

I noticed that the sleeping portion of the room had an adjoining room, there was a large television protected by Plexiglas and about six to eight metal picnic type tables. I soon learned that we were to eat and sleep in this confined area. So where were the restrooms?

Restrooms? I told you I was naïve. The toilet was on the other end of the sleep room divided by a half wall so that when you squatted or sat your head was above the wall, everyone else in the room could see, hear and smell what ever you did on the other side of that wall. There was one sink next to the toilet and one shower. This was not going to be easy for me. I kept waiting to hear them call my name to let me know I was being released but it did not happen.

I noticed a phone on the wall you could only make collect calls of course because there was no money allowed in the room. I called my mother. When she said, "Oh baby, are you alright?" The tears started again. I believe I asked, "What was going on and when am I getting out of here?" My mother explained that the lawyer was very upset with the judge for the decision that was made. She went on to explain that if the lawyer had been aware that this was going to happen to me, he would have never allowed me to go to the courthouse and that he had tried unsuccessfully to have me released that day. She said, "Unfortunately baby, you have to stay there until you go to court on Wednesday." I said, "No, Mommy, NO!" Then I returned like a soldier to my quiet state and I wiped my tears and said with as much conviction as possible, "Don't worry about me, I'll be okay." (You know, that life with a smile mask back on. I just feel that when I am at my lowest, I cannot unload that on others. I refuse to allow others to feel sorry for me or hurt for me. I will bear it alone, with the help of the Lord.)

The Lord, where was He now? I was beginning to know what Jonah felt like in the belly of the whale. There was a difference, however, I was not running from what the Lord had told me to do, at least not that I was conscience of. Once again, I was angry with God. I said to myself that I would not pray. But much like Jeremiah, it was like fire shut up in my bones and I found myself announcing, "I'll be having circle prayer at about 9:00 pm if anyone is interested." (To my amazement, those words came out strongly and without tears.) At prayer time, there were four women including myself, I sang a song of praise and we bowed our heads in prayer. I was finally at rest.

Following prayer, I sat at one of the tables and watched the ten o'clock news. A few of the women that witnessed the prayer and the ones that joined in prayer gathered at the table and asked me why I was there. I explained that I had been accused of hurting a child in my care and that I was facing several felony charges of child endangerment and few misdemeanor charges as well. Then one of the women said, "There is something different about you, what is it?" I wasn't sure that I wanted to reveal that I was a preacher. I did not want the women to feel that I believed that I was any better than they were. One after one they started saying and asking, "Yeah, you are different. What is it about you?" I took a long deep breath and I said, "Well, I am an ordained minister."

I heard the whispers around the room, "Did she say that she's a preacher?" Some were saying, "We don't need no more of that God sh_t in here." Others were intrigued. Many had never met or heard of a woman preacher. Many had questions, others wanted personal prayer and still others just wanted to protect me.

Remember, I had never been issued a towel, somehow one appeared on my bunk and it was clean (I mean white). I was a little leery, I had heard that you have to be careful about inmates wanting to help or protect you. I did not want to revert to my violent past; I did not want to become a real inmate. God must have been protecting me, because everyone that came to my aid did so only out of pure intent.

I was somewhat surprised to find out that the lights were not turned off or down at night. They remained at full brightness twenty four-seven. I guess if you turn the lights off you run the risk of more mischief. With the lights on the cameras can pick up any trouble brewing. At an adjacent cell trouble did brew. We heard the sirens and the guards running down the halls. Many of the women ran to the doors to see if the could see out. They were unsuccessful. We later found out that two women had gotten into a fistfight. We found out because the troublemaker was reassigned to our cell. Now, I was really praying!

CHAPTER TWENTY-FIVE

I dosed off and on in ten to twenty minutes increments through out the first night. I was listening to the sounds and many women did not sleep at night, they roamed the room and talked about their street lives (conversations I could have lived without hearing—once again I was thankful for my sheltered life).

I learned from the night talks that the shower only works from 4:00 am until 7:00 am and those going to court get to shower first then it is first come first serve. Now if I knew anything, I knew that I was going to take a shower. It was bad enough that I had to sleep in the clothing provided by the county because of my undergarments being confiscated, I was sweaty and nasty and I was going to get in that shower.

I was able to get into the shower, I had to use my hands to bathe and someone had given me soap and allowed me to use their deodorant. There wasn't much I could do to my hair without a comb or brush so I just let the water run through it and styled it as best I could with my fingers. This was one time I was happy that the grade of my hair allows water to curl it. I knew without styling foam or lotion it would be wild by the end of the day but for now this would work. The shower it self was small, I am slightly overweight, (I could stand to lose forty pounds) and I could not turn in that shower. I had to stand in one position to wash myself. If I needed to turn, it would require me to expose some portion of my body outside of the shower and if it were in my ability that was not going to happen.

I had no underclothing so I had to put back on my smelly "prison wear". I was startled when my name was called around 10:00 am. I went to the door to show my bracelet proving my identity, I was handed a small paper bag through the opening that was used to serve us our meals. I was excited to find, one white wireless bra and one pair of white underwear. The bra was the right size it was one of my sports bras from home that I had not yet opened. The panties on the other hand were huge (please forgive me my larger sisters, but I was wearing a size 10 in dresses at the time) they were a size 10. The underwear came up to my neck, but I put them on, they were clean and new.

(For the life of me, I could not understand, why the man I have been married to for nearly seven years would not know what size underwear to buy me and why was there only one pair?)

I spent the entire day confined to these two adjacent rooms being observant and as quiet as possible. I called my mother and my sister, Celeste. I called my daughter but I did not want to burden her. I called my friend Wanda. I was never able to reach my husband by phone. That evening Wanda came to visit me using her minister license. She informed me that she would be in court the next morning and that she would bail me out. She let me know that she had discussed it with her husband and if it meant getting a second mortgage on their home, they would make sure I did not have to spend a third night in jail. (I had already learned from speaking with my mother that my husband had informed them that he did not have the money to get me out and that I would have to stay there until the following Monday, allowing him time to get the money. He had surely, lost his mind!)

Wanda told me how much she loved me and assured me that she and her congregation were holding me up in prayer. She told me not to worry that everything would be all right.

When I returned to the cell, I was told that the guards had come looking for me and they had a package for me. I called for the guard and I was given a small paper bag with two more pair of size 10 underwear. At this point I did not care about the size I knew that I would have clean underclothes for court the next morning. I scrubbed the underclothes I had been wearing in the sink, I planned to use them as wash clothe the next morning when my opportunity to shower came.

I had circle prayer this time our circle grew to about six women. After prayer several of the women asked me to speak with them individually. I listened to their stories and their fears. Some told of their drug habits and the vicious cycle of prostitution to support their habits. Some told me why others were there and requested that I pray for the ones they told me about. Others were just dumb founded as to how anyone might believe that I could have hurt a child. I told them all that I would pray for them. I asked them if they truly believed in the power of prayer, to pray for me as well. I encouraged them as much as I could.

I pleaded with those with children to change their ways and attempt to provide stable homes for their children. There were several of these women that left lasting impressions in my mind and heart. One young lady was there because she left her infant with her violent boyfriend and he killed her baby. She was just a baby herself barely eighteen, her mother died when she was young and her father lived in another state. She had been bounced around throughout her family and foster homes. She was yearning for a mother's love. I held her in my arms and I just let her cry. I told her that I loved her but most importantly that God loved her. I told her that I would keep her in my prayers and I have to this day. I told her I would write her, I did but the letters came back as addressee not known.

There was another that resembled my daughter but she was slightly older than my child. She was one of my protectors: she traded foods with me. I have very strict dietary laws and she would give me her cereal for my bacon. She gave me white T-shirts to cover my underclothing so that I could remove the stinky workhouse issued garments. She never joined the circle prayers but I am positive I saw her bow her head and wipe a tear when we prayed. She had thirty days to serve and she promised me that she would stay on the straight path. She was convinced that the revolving door of the county workhouse was not the life for her. She told me that many of the women there were always there for one reason or another and she was not going to allow that to be her story. I promised her that I would write her and that she would always have a special place in my heart for the kindness she had shown me. I wrote her, she never wrote back.

Then there was the lesbian prostitute. She slept during the day and kept everyone else up at night. To the best of my ability, I ignored her conversations. They were perverse and deviant. She was in my opinion one of the demons of the cellblock and I had to tell her so my last night there. Everyone was tired many of us had to get up at the 4 am wake-up to prepare for court. At about midnight, I sat straight up in my bed looked her in the face (her bunk was a top one also and her head faced my feet) and said, "Satan, shut-up and go to sleep!" Then I laid down placed my towel over my face to shield out some of the light and asked the Lord to let me sleep.

The next morning she was sure to tell me. She said, "Hey, did you know that you called me Satan and told me to shut-up and go to sleep?" I said, "Did you shut-up?" She replied, "yes." I asked, "Did you go to sleep?" She again answered, "yes." So I replied, "Then apparently I was talking to the right person!" Everyone in the cellblock laughed including the demon child.

Then there was the educated prostitute. She waited until Wednesday morning to decide to talk to me. She asked me if I would come to her bunk to talk with her. She had the only single bed in the room. I sat down at the foot of her bed as she began to pour out her heart. I was touched, I was overwhelmed with love and compassion, and this must have been how Jesus felt when the women caught in adultery was brought to him. She told me how she was the valedictorian of her high school class and voted most likely to succeed. She told me of her full scholarship to college and the degrees she had obtained. She told me of the high paying corporate job she once had. She told me about and shared with me pictures of her beautiful children, some drug babies, being raised by her aging mother. She told me of her beginnings in the church and of how she was introduced to drinking and drugs. (But by Grace, their go I!)

She told me that she was tired; she told me that she wanted to change. She had been given the option of being released or remaining in jail until she could be put into a residential treatment center. She revealed how she toiled with the decision and opted to remain so that she could get the help the she so earnestly needed. I held her hands as she shared her life. I shared some of my painful past with her. We prayed, I asked God to deliver her from the demon of drugs and to return her to His loving care.

What touched me most was her expression of love. She took my face into both her hands and said, "You may not know why God allowed you to be here, but I do. You are here for me. I needed you. God knew I needed you, so He sent you to me." She went on to say, "Your work is done, don't worry you're going home today." We embraced and we never spoke again.

I was called to leave for court.

109

CHAPTER TWENTY-SIX

We were lined up in the hallway with our backs against the walls each waiting to be frisked and then led away like sheep to the slaughter. I had butterflies in my stomach. I did not know what to expect and quite frankly, I was scared stiff.

I was not sure what to say or what was going to be required to say and/or do. I knew the truth, but so far other than my attorney no one seemed willing to listen. I kept hearing myself repeat in my head, "But when they deliver you up, take no thought how or what ye shall speak: for it shall be given you in that same hour what ye shall speak." (Matthew 10:19)

Once again, I found myself in shackles, hands and feet. This time we traveled by bus not by van. The bus looked like a school bus except that it was gray and had bars on the doors and windows and a metal gate to separate the passengers from the driver. In the center of the bus was a gated fence to separate half the passengers I was curious about what its purpose was. It didn't take long for me to find out, after the women were put on the rear of the bus and the gate closed and locked, men were loaded on to the bus.

We were given strict instructions: there was to be no communication or contact between the men and the women, anyone violating these instructions would not receive their day in court and would be returned to the work house on the next bus. Most of the women riders adhered to the instructions. There was a couple on the bus that had not seen each other since they were locked up, it had been about 21 days and they were screaming back and forth to one another. It was quite annoying but in a small way touching. They were warned and threaten but they just kept on going right up to the time that we reached the courthouse and as promised they were not allowed to appear in court. They were placed in separate cells at opposite ends of a long hallway and they kept up their yells of endearing love until we were put on to an elevator and led up to another holding cell.

The wait before going into court seemed endless. We arrived at the courthouse probably between 6:45 and 7:00 am and we sat in a cell only shackled by our legs. There was some interaction but not much until I offered to have prayer. By this time almost all of the women in the holding cell were aware of my situation and that I was a preacher. Apparently word travels fast in lock up. Everyone was willing to have prayer so we all stood locked hands and I prayed. I prayed for the guilty, that God would forgive them and search their hearts; I prayed that if God found them in a repentant state, that the judge be merciful towards them. I prayed for the innocent that they might be released and I prayed that whatever God's will was that we would all accept it with grace. I cried for the innocent, I cried for the victims but I did not cry for myself (not this time). My only request of God was not uttered out loud; it was that some soul might have been reached by my presence and that I might be able to go home, if it was in His will.

After what seemed liked hours passed, I was finally called into court. We went in by two's shackled by our arms and legs we each had one free hand. As soon as I stepped into the courtroom, I saw my mother's face. I wanted to smile but the experiences of the past few days would not allow a smile to peak through. I must have looked like a common criminal to everyone there. One of my fellow cellmates had braided my hair so that it would not be standing all over my head: I was in my workhouse orange and chained to another inmate. I could see the sadness and pain on the face of my mother and I hurt for her. My sorrow and pain no longer mattered. I sat in silence until my name was called and I stood to my feet as was required.

I listened intently as the charges against me were read. I was being accused of two felony counts of child endangerment/abuse and misdemeanor charge of child endangerment. What I heard read was considerably different than what the Dublin police had told me back in January and the details blew me away.

The Dublin police had told me that the parents took the child to the emergency room immediately after leaving my home, but the report read in open court stated that they went to the emergency room around 8:00 pm. My mind was racing. I was perplexed. What happened to the child during the three hour time period after they left my home? Now, I was seeing things differently. Not only had the police lied to me, but I also, now felt as though I had been set up. Had the accident

111

that occurred in my home afforded the parents an opportunity to make false allegations against me?

When I heard the amount of my bail my knees went weak. I was praying that Wanda was going to be able to pay it without too much hardship on her family. Mad Dog was not in court that morning he was out of the country and had sent an associate to stand in his place. The attorney informed me that I would be released that evening and that there would be papers for me to sign. With that I was whisked away back to a holding cell.

By now my stomach was growling. We were brought sandwiches but I was unable to eat them, it was pork bologna. I probably did not mention earlier that I do not eat pork for religious reasons and I am deathly allergic as well. Fortunately, the guards did not frisk me as aggressively as usual and I had been able to conceal leftovers from dinner the night before in my bra. (Now I know some of you are wondering how could I possibly conceal food in my bra?) It is amazing what you learn in lock up. For once having no cleavage between size 38DD breasts paid off. (I later learned that the inmates had also informed the guards that I was a minister. This explained why they were a little gentler during their search of me. It is amazing how God works.) My small stash took the edge off and then one of my cellmates informed me that I could ask the guard for a diabetic's lunch. I did and I was given an apple and milk. Once again the Lord was looking out for me.

We waited until about 4:00 pm and then those being released were taken to sign the bail papers and informed of the conditions of bail. We were then transported back to the workhouse, again with the men on one half of the bus and the women on the other. Upon arrival back at the workhouse the women remained on the bus until the men were searched and sent to their cells, then we were carted off the bus for the dreaded frisking once again. Again, the guard was quiet gentle with me and kept saying, "it's almost over, I need to touch you here, I will now touch you here, okay it's over you did good". Since I was not yet in the knowledge of my cell mates informing the guards of my calling, I thought this treatment was strange but I was not complaining, I was tired of being man handled.

I was anxious when I got back to the cellblock. I packed up my things and made sure I had all the belongings needed to get out. Cup check, spoon check, towel check (thanks to another inmate), washcloth check and I put them all into the pillowcase and prepared my mat for the transport. I gave my underclothing to the some of the woman that were going to be staying for a while. Some one mentioned that the guards had been by again looking for me while I was at court. When I asked one of the guards about it she said she had no idea why someone was looking for me.

I waited for an opportunity to use the phone. I called my mother. She updated me on the events of the day, told me that my bail had been paid and that they were told I would be released between 5:00 and 6:00 pm. Wanda would pick me up if I needed her to and I was to call her as soon as I was released.

Dinner came and still no word on my release. Some names were called but mine was not one of them. I was praying that nothing had gone wrong. It was eight by the time I was finally called for release; I knew the time because the prime time line up had just started on television. When I reached the hallway one other woman being released met me.

We were given our belongings after signing for them and then led to a holding cell where we could put on our street clothes for release. After about a half-hour passed the other woman was released but I was left in the holding cell. I kept hearing the guards say my name but they never came back to the cell. I was beginning to wonder if they had forgotten about me, but afraid to call out for fear of some type of additional punishment. My claustrophobia was getting the better of me, so I just prayed silently and began to sing.

Hours passed and I was still alone in this cell. I could hear the phone ringing at the guard's station and I could here them call my married name, but they never came to my cell. My stomach was really acting up by now, partly due to my nervousness and partly due to my not having any of my medications during my stay. I wanted to use the toilet in the cell and at the same time was afraid some one would come in as soon as I squatted. My stomach won this battle. I reluctantly went to use the toilet. No one came; I sat for at least another hour before someone returned.

They finally, let me go and I heard some grumbling behind the desk. "Don't know what that is about," I thought, but I was just relieved to know that I was going to be free. When I reached the outside doors, I took a deep breath and looked around, I did not see anyone there to pick me up. I looked for the phone and I called home, no answer. I tried Wanda, no answer.

I went outside and stood for a few minutes looking around, still no one. I went back in and sat patiently. About ten minutes later my husband came into the lobby, he said he had been there since he left work that evening and did not understand why it took me so long to come out. There was no embrace, no questions as to how I was, just complaints about his inconvenience.

He went on to tell me that he had been calling the guard's station every thirty minutes since 6:00 pm in order to find out when they would be releasing me and expressed how nasty the guards had been to him. (Imagine that! He was on the outside and they were nasty to him. Does he even hear himself? I was on the inside for three days! Does he think they were nice to me?) Now, it was clear to me. I knew why I kept hearing my name when the phone rang and why I was held so much longer than the other woman. I was being punished for my husband's actions. I said nothing.

He had brought my purse with him so I starting searching for my medication, he asked what I was looking for and before I could answer my cell phone rang. It was Wanda; she just wanted to know if I was okay and to make sure that I had been picked up. She informed me that she was actually on her way to pick me up. I let her know it was not necessary and thanked her for all she had done.

When I finished the call, I asked Pastor where my medicine was. He got angry. He said, "Didn't you get your medicine from the jail? I took it there this morning before going to court." I calmly said, "no, I did not know that you brought my medicine." Then he said angrily, "So they never gave you the medicine? What was the purpose of me rushing all the way there this morning if they weren't going to give you the medicine? Now I guess we have to go all the way back, just to pick it up, huh?"

I was hurting inside, I was furious! If he could see how I was feeling or hear what I was thinking, he would back off. I took a deep breath and said, "Yes, we need to go back, I have not had my meds for three days and my body is beginning to react." If he only knew how much I did not want to go back. I never wanted to see that place again. When we arrived there was no one in the security booth. The sign said "Back in 30 minutes". I was unaware of how far into the thirty minutes it was so I just waited. A guard passing by asked why we were there. I explained that I had just been released and that my husband had delivered my medication earlier that morning. I was asked what types of medications. I began to list them by name and what they were for: High blood pressure, high cholesterol, acid reflux, estrogen, and allergies. The guard then replied, "Oh you were in the medical ward, why didn't they give you your medication when you left."

I explained that I was not in the medical ward. I was then informed that based on my medical history I should not have been in general population. A lot of consolation that knowledge was now, the bottom line was I needed my medication. The guard called the nurses station and was told there was no medication there for me. Then I remembered the women telling me that a guard had been looking for me earlier that day. Could that guard have been a nurse bringing me my medication? I mentioned this to the guard, he made another phone call and we waited.

I was right, the guard had been a nurse and the reason why they were unable to find my prescriptions was because she had once again gone looking to give me the medications and transfer me to the medical ward. The bag was brought down and I was finally getting out of there, for good this time.

I was exhausted and hungry but with his mood, I was not asking for anything. It was now almost midnight and he had been inconvenienced enough!

Life With A Smile

I walked silently into the house; my first stop was the shower. I grabbed a sandwich and something to drink. (I don't remember what.) I had not slept in the same room or the same bed with Pastor since January, but I was afraid to be alone and I told him so, so I grabbed my pillows from the room down the hall and eased into the bed with him.

CHAPTER TWENTY-SEVEN

I guess my fatigue was greater than I realized. I am not sure that I went to sleep. I may have passed out. I never heard a thing. I awoke about 10:00 am, alone!

When I awoke I was shaking uncontrollably. The ordeal I had experienced was more than I could handle. I could not seem to pull myself together. Being alone was not good. I felt as though I was losing my mind. I guess I can understand what a caged animal feels like when it is released. I did not know what to do or what not to do. I could not think. My mind seemed to have shut down.

I recall going to the bathroom. I remember screaming, "Jesus help me!" at the top of my lungs. I don't remember getting the telephone, I don't even remember dialing the number, I just remember hearing my mother's voice and sobbing like a baby, "somebody help me, Jesus help me, please somebody help me!"

My voice must have been distorted from the cries and screams, because my mother said who is this. I tried to get out my name, "Wy. Wy.., Wynette." I heard her voice, "Oh Nette, where are you baby?" I don't know if I answered her, I do know that I just kept calling Jesus. I think I heard her say she was sending Celeste over and that she and my father were getting in their car and would be getting to Columbus as fast as they could.

I don't know what I did next. I may have passed out again. I remember feeling the arms of my sister, Celeste around me. I remember her crying and pleading with me not to cry. I remember her caress. I remember her telling me that I was the strong one. I was the one that instructed her in the love of God. I remember her saying, "How do you expect me to get saved or trust God if you don't?"

Those must have been the words I needed. I remember that my crying quieted. I was still shaking and confused but I was able to shower and get dressed. I don't remember if I combed my hair or if Celeste did. Celeste forced me to eat and Mommy and Daddy arrived. Celeste must have packed my things, I don't remember doing it. My parents decided

117

to take me back to Cleveland with them. (It was apparent that Pastor did not know what I needed, nor did he seem to care. If he had he would have never left me there alone. In all fairness, he was hurting also, he had just found out that I had filed for divorce.)

My parents thought it best if they take my car to Cleveland, as well; I would need to come home when I felt stronger. So they took me to Cleveland and nurtured me until I was able to be in a room alone without freaking out. By Sunday, I was well enough to drive myself home.

I knew that I would not be there long. I could not stand the sight of Pastor, at this point. His treatment of me following my release and his explanation for not visiting me while I was locked-up was unacceptable. He told me, that since I was using both my maiden and married names, visiting day wasn't until Thursday and that I was released on Wednesday. When I said to him, "Pastor, you are not only my husband but a minister, as a minister you could have come all day everyday." He then responded, "When I wanted to come, Wanda was there." (So which was true, the visiting day or the visit from another minister?) This was the type of double talk I was sick of! He made me so angry I could spit. I actually had visions of punching him in his face! (Now, I knew that these feelings were not of God, that is why I knew I had to get out of there and fast!)

He tried to talk me out of divorce, but he could not give me any reasons other than financial ones as to why I should stay. The financial aspects did not benefit me and even if they would have, money would and could not have kept me there, at this point. I had already closed the daycare and said my goodbyes to the parents and children. I had given away and sold off all of my toys and children's furniture. My daughter had her own place and had just had her second child. My son was in Cleveland. Celeste and her daughters had found a place and Celeste had enrolled in community college. I had no reason to stay, I had made up my mind, and I was out!

I contacted Mad Dog to make sure that all my legal papers were in order for me to move and I was assured that it would be fine as long as I did not miss any of my court dates. Mad Dog also informed me that he had referred my criminal case to another attorney. He was devastated by the events that led to my arrest and knew that he was in above his head. He was a domestic attorney not a criminal attorney and he wanted me to have the best possible representation. I respected him for that decision and I called to arrange an appointment with the criminal attorney.

I was in the process of renting a truck in order to move. I had no idea how I was going to load the truck when I received a telephone call from a childhood friend and church member from Cleveland. ("God works in mysterious ways." I had often heard this statement but now I was living it.) I had told her that I really didn't have time to talk because I was trying to move back to Cleveland and was attempting to locate help to load my truck. I did not want to enlist the help of any of the local church congregation because I felt it would be a conflict of interest on their behalf and I did not want anyone to inform Pastor of my intent. She said, "Give me a few minutes and I will call you right back."

When the phone rang again she informed me that she had relatives in the Columbus area that were on their way to help me and they would accept any monetary gift I would give them. She was sending four men. I told her I only had enough money for the truck rental and gas and I might be able to scrape up another $50 if I had enough room on my credit card to cover the gas. She said it did not matter to them. They were going to help me just because she asked them to.

These men worked untiringly from about 9:00 am until 4:00pm. I gave them what food and drink I had in the house and I was able to stretch the $50 to $80. They loaded my entire house and I was able to leave before my husband returned home from work. It was the third of July and I knew that he would be off for the Holiday the next day. I could not afford to delay my escape.

I had been moving small things to storage in Cleveland prior to the big move. There were boxes all over the house. I did not try to hide them. It was amazing to me that Pastor said he had no idea I was leaving. (Apparently, he must be blind.) When I left I removed everything from the house with the exception of the marital bed (I had no desire to sleep in a bed I had shared with him for so many years), one nightstand (which he had broken by over stuffing), the small refrigerator I had previously purchased and used for the daycare, his desktop and laptop computers and the fax machine. I left him some linen and all of his clothing and personal items. I left the family portraits but I took everything else, yes everything!

Initially, it was difficult to find work. I had been out of the traditional work force for four full years and many potential employers were of the belief that my skills were diminished. They did not completely understand that I ran a business. It was not a fly-by-night babysitting service. I used *QuickBooks Pro* for the financial aspect of the business. I had monthly and eventually quarterly newsletters. I used a *Microsoft Access* program for another portion of my business, my skills were anything but rusty, but I understood their concerns.

I worked many part-time and temporary positions. I even worked one position from 7:00 pm to 7:00 am for a two-week period. I am surprised I survived that one (remember I can not sleep in the daylight). I worked through temporary employment agencies and I sold off my belongings to survive. I received my first break when the same childhood friend that sent me movers, referred me to an associate of hers for an executive secretarial position. I was not thrilled with the idea of being someone's secretary but I really needed the work so I submitted my resume and went in for the interview. I was hired on the spot and began working immediately. I was the Executive Secretary to the Imperial Potentate of the Shriner's.

I will not say much about that position other than it did help to pay my bills. It would take another whole book to describe that experience, but if you have ever watched the Flintstones' episodes when Fred and Barney went to the Lodge, it wasn't much different. I will describe it in one word **Chauvinistic**. I was determined to do a great job and I did, but the appreciation or recognition was never given. The best part about the job was that I wasn't given a hard time about my court dates in Columbus. I had made my employer aware that I was in the midst of a bitter divorce; I did not reveal the other (criminal) legal matter I was battling. I remained in this position from September until the end of December.

CHAPTER TWENTY-EIGHT

I was not happy in my position but I was not looking for additional work. At the time, I was content working there because of the flexibility of my court travel. In October, while I was yet employed with the Shriner's, my legal battle with regard to the child abuse allegations was finalized and at the advise of my attorney I had plead guilty to a lesser charge of attempted child endangerment. The plus side was that the five to fifteen years I was facing in prison was converted to two years of probation or parole. The minus side was that I now had a felony conviction. Because I was already employed at the time of the conviction I was not required to inform my employer, however, I would need to inform any potential new employers.

Arrangements had been made to transfer my case to the Cleveland area authorities and I would have to report to a parole officer within the next month. I would also need to complete anger management and parenting courses. If I was angry, I surely felt justified, but I was determined to do whatever the courts required to clear my name.

In early December, I stopped by Angie's house one Saturday to pick up some of my belongings. I had stored some of my things at her home and I spent some weeknights and most weekends at her house. (My parents' house is busy; sometimes I just needed to get away.) Angie was asleep but she awoke to tell me that she had a job for me. I thought she needed me to do something for her so I asked. "What do you need?" Her reply was, "No, I mean I really have a job for you."

Angie told me of an associate of her employer that was looking for an administrative assistant. Angie has held the position of administrative assistant to her employer for more than twelve years and had told this associate about me and he wanted to see my resume. I wasn't very optimistic. I'd had leads before and they were never very positive. I was afraid that once my criminal history was revealed that I would be denied the opportunity. I reluctantly agreed to forward my resume and a cover letter to Angie the following Monday so that she might forward it to her associate.

Angie called me and I could hear the excitement in her voice, "He was really impressed," she said, "he will be calling you tonight!" I said, "Okay, I will expect his call." He did not call. I was a little disappointed but I thought maybe God did not intend for me to move at this point, after all I was still going to need to travel to finalize this divorce. The next morning Angie called me at work to see if I had received the call. I told her that I had not and not to worry about it, I would continue in my current position. Angie took it upon herself to follow-up and find out if there was some reason I did not get the call the previous evening. She called back to say that I would definitely be getting a call that day.

When I returned home, I had not one call but two from the potential employer requesting that I call back that evening no matter how late to arrange for an interview. I called and spoke with the gentleman and arranged an interview for the next evening as not to interfere with my then current employment. We must have spoke for nearly an hour and by the end of the conversation I was not only going to be interviewed the following evening but also attending a Cleveland Cavaliers game.

I was a little apprehensive about the interview, but mostly about the game attendance. What had I gotten myself into? I had never had an interview that ended in entertainment, but I trusted Angie and I knew she would never allow me to be placed in a position of potential harm. (She was the one person who knew all my little secrets.) When I hung up from the call, I immediately called Angie. She reassured me that everything was on the up and up and that I should relax, be myself and go for the job.

The interview went well and the game was great. The Cavs won. I was still uneasy, I had not informed him of my conviction. I did not know when it would be the best time to do so. If he were interested in employing me I would have no choice. In the car, on the ride back to my car, I just let it out.

I began by saying something like, "There is something I think you need to know about me." I went on to tell him briefly of the ordeal and his response to my complete surprise was. "I appreciate your honesty, this will have no bearing on my decision." He went on to say, "We all go

122

through things in our lives that we are not completely proud of. I just want you to know that this too will pass."

Wow, I thought. This guy amazingly understands or I just blew the interview. Well, I did not blow the interview, the next morning he called to arrange a second interview so that I might meet his partner and the director of sales. I was to come in the next morning, Friday, prior to my scheduled working hours.

The interviews went overtime. I was asked to take some tests. I arrived back at work an hour late. As I sat down to my desk the telephone was ringing. The voice on the other end said, "Wynette?" I answered, "speaking." He went on, "I was going to wait until later this afternoon, probably around 4:00 pm to make this call, but I knew when you left here that I was going to offer you the position so why make you wait? If you are interested I would like for you to begin in two weeks." He was going to fax me over an offer letter to sign and fax back. (He was aware of my impending divorce and had no problem with my needing time off to travel to Columbus for my court appointments.) The starting salary was approximately $6,000 less a year than I grossed when I was self-employed but it was $6,000 more than I was making at the time. (Good looking out, Angie! You know I love you, Ace!)

Do you see how God works? He is truly amazing!

I enrolled in my required classes. I was to attend anger management classes every Monday for nine weeks and through a different program, parenting classes were twice a week, Wednesday and Saturday, for eight weeks.

CHAPTER TWENTY-NINE

All of the traveling up and down Interstate 71 going to and from Cleveland to Columbus was wearing on me mentally, emotionally and physically. I did my best not to complain. My family, especially Daddy, knew what I was enduring. I was careful about what friends I would let know my pain. I did not want to be a burden on others. I was an emotional basket case.

Although the court travel for the criminal case was over, I was still in the emotional battle of my life with the divorce case. Pastor was determined to play hardball. When I initially filed for divorce I asked only to keep the items I left with and to have one year of financial support in the amount of $800 a month. He said and I quote, "I will do and say, whatever I have to do or say to make sure that you do not get a dime! We have not even been married for ten years and you do not deserve anything!"

He was true to his word, he brought up the criminal case sighting that he should not have to provide me money to defend myself from the charges. He mentioned in court documents that I was not making enough money to support myself because I only had a high school education and I was not applying myself. I could go on but it makes me beyond angry to discuss it. (If you haven't figured it out by now, if you push me into a corner, I will come out fighting!)

I truly had about enough so I unleashed Mad Dog. I told him, "You know the legal system better than I do, do what needs to be done." So the court battle and the traveling continued. In the mean time I had to go to the court ordered classes. I had not kept Pastor abreast of the outcome of that case, so unless he did some checking on his own he would have no idea of what had occurred. I was praying that he would not attempt to use the outcome of my criminal case against me. (He did not.)

To say that I was fatigued would be an understatement. I was working full time, attending classes three nights a week and attending my regular weeknight church services. I would leave Wednesday night's class and head to church. I kept smiling, it has been my life's mask,

124

but on the inside I was dying. I was having trouble with my faith. I did not want to preach. I told my pastor, "How can you expect me to get up and tell the congregation to put their faith and trust in God, when I am having a difficult time trusting Him myself?"

I am so grateful for the encouraging words and the prayers that were offered up for me. I am a true believer in "The effectual fervent prayer of a righteous man availeth much." I need to give special thanks to those that pushed me, when I did not want to be pushed and to those that admonished and rebuked me when I was beginning to stray from the Lord.

Stephanie without your loving encouragement and your nagging reminders of my faith, calling and vows to God, I do not know where I would be right now. Thank you! Please know that I will love you forever.

San, you may not have known it but you said just what I needed to hear when I needed to hear it. Even though I may have wanted to hit you for it. Thank you!

Gena, although your encouragement may not have been from the scripture, I realize that I needed you as well to get through. God has His way of putting just the right people in your life and path just when you need them.

Mommy, or should I say my pastor, I was angry with you when you pushed me to preach, but as usual you were right. I remember the words you spoke before calling me to speak the faithful Sunday morning. "I know that this minister has been going through some tough trials and I had agreed not to call her to speak, however I felt that I could no longer allow her to sit silent. I did not call her to preach, God did, she has a job to do and she must do it." I also remember my sermon. I believe I cried through the entire delivery.

My subject was, "No More Lying By the Pool," and my text scripture was St. John 5:1-9.

Life With A Smile

As I began to elaborate on the theme, I realized that God was talking to me, more than I was talking to His people. I began by explaining how many people live in a façade. They present an appearance of health and well-being when most of them are hurting and/or broken. As I opened up the scripture to discuss the man that had been unable to walk for thirty-eight years and was waiting for his opportunity to step into the healing pool only to miss his chance when someone else would reach the troubling waters before him each year, I began to see myself. I was waiting for a miracle when the miracle was always right there around me, if only I would reach out for it. I needed to, *rise, take up my bed and walk*! Whoa, what deliverance I received. I pray that someone else was edified, but I am humbled and thankful for the deliverance God gave me.

If you think that everything was perfect for me after this revelation, think again. For me it was momentary, but God was not through with me yet. My next sermon topic was: "The Gates of Hell Shall Not Prevail." God was reassuring me that He would not allow Satan to destroy me, no matter the avenue he decided to use and believe me he had some tricks up his sleeve.

The divorce was finalized on May 29th almost a full year after I filed. Pastor could keep his dime, because the courts ordered that he pay me support for three years. I will not reveal the amounts but I was also awarded a substantial amount of his retirement. I guess he is now aware of what a high school education can do for you when you apply yourself. (Those words will probably haunt him forever!) I would return to the annual national church convention with my maiden name. I did not want to be called by that man's name. I feel strongly that one day his ship is going to sink and I did and do not want to be aboard when it happens.

I had completed my court ordered classes. Well, if the truth were told, I ended up facilitating more classes than I was a student of. (I am still actively involved with the program in which I took Parenting Classes. I am on the Board of Directors, I oversee the Parenting Program, and I am the Intake Coordinator and Personnel Director all on a voluntary basis.) You see what Satan meant for my bad, God meant for my good. I have been exposed to more hurting people than I could ever imagine,

126

male and female, and I am humbled that God would count me worthy
to aid in the restoration of His people.

I still had to report to a probation officer. God's hand was clearly seen
there, as well. On my first visit (I was to report monthly), I was sent
for the drug testing. I passed, of course, and was told when I returned
the following month that I would only need to report every three
months. I was not permitted to leave the state without written
permission. This was a struggle for me because; I am accustomed to
traveling for church events. My probation officer never denied me
traveling privileges. I still struggled with this because it was the
knowing that I could not decide to get up on a Saturday morning and
drive to the outlet mall in neighboring Pennsylvania or take a weekend
shopping trip to New York City. I silently cried when my mother and
sisters would go without me. I knew that it was a small sacrifice, I was
free; I was not in jail!

To add insult to injury, after living on the third floor of my parents'
house for nearly a year, I was told that my youngest sister was having
some problems with her marriage and needed to come home with her
twin babies. One of the conditions of my probation prohibited me from
cohabitating with small children. My family had no fears or concerns
for the safety of the girls. (Of course, they had no reason to.) But for
me, after spending three days in jail, I was not taking any chances on
violating probation and having to return to a worse place than I had
already been. I needed a place to live and I had no means by which to
pay rent due to my outstanding legal fees and credit card debt. (I had
lived off my credit cards when I wasn't working.)

My feelings were hurt. I felt as though I was being pushed out of the
nest without wings. I had never felt in my life like my mother had
treated me like a stepchild, but now I did. I felt as though, she was
choosing one child over another and it cut like a knife. I was not upset
with my sister. She had just graduated from college and had not yet
found employment and she had twin babies. If someone had to struggle
it should not be her, but what was I supposed to do?

How many of my readers believe that God always has a ram in the
bush, even when you don't see it? Well, He does and He did for me.

Life With A Smile

In a conversation with Big Archie, I had explained my situation and my desperation. Archie was living at his parents' home, with his mother and our son. His father had passed away in March and his mother needed assistance and our son needed a parent in the home. The other house owned by his parents, the one Archie had previously been living in was empty. He said I could live there rent-free on the condition that I clean it up. I agreed and three days later, on the first Sunday in July, I moved into the house and my sister moved in with my parents.

CHAPTER THIRTY

When I tell you that I had no idea what I had just gotten myself into you would not be able to completely understand unless you had seen it for yourself. "You will have to clean it up," he said. Why didn't he just tell me to call the fire department after I lit a match? I literally had to make a path to enter the house to bring in my belongings.

There was wall-to-wall junk. Bags, boxes and papers were everywhere. You see Archie had not spent much time at home due to his father's illness. Archie is also an income tax consultant, so it was difficult to determine what was trash. The beds were buried in clothing. I just wanted a dump truck and an exterminator. My first night in the house I had no choice but to clean one of the bedrooms so that I could sleep. I scrubbed and I scrapped. I sprayed and I prayed and around 2:00 am the bedroom was clean enough to sleep in. (Of course, I used Lysol and Febreze on the mattress and let it air out before considering placing my sheets, let alone placing my body, on it. You can also believe that I used the thickest mattress cover I owned.)

Each night when I returned home from work, I busied myself with cleaning. I am claustrophobic, remember, so there was no way I could stay in the house the way it was. The very thought that there might be something living in the house other than me made me crazy. So my bedtime was between 2:00 and 3:00 am for about a month.

My first tasks were the bedroom I was to sleep in, the kitchen and the bathrooms. These were completely clean in the first three days. The other rooms, I did a little at time, boxing things and aligning the boxes along the walls in the dining room and storing what I could in the attic and basement. I probably did not tell you that it is a four-bedroom house with two bathrooms (one on the second floor and one in the basement). It is an older home and very large. There is to this day still one room that I have not been able to organize; it is Big Archie's former (and I guess current) office. I gave up on that room except for the closet; I have a lot of clothes so I cleared the closet for my use.

So my need for housing was fulfilled. If you believe this made everything better, think again. I have never lived alone in my life. I come from a family of nine children. I was married and had my first child within a year after graduating from high school. I have always been someone's daughter, wife or mother. A month before turning 26 for the sixteenth time, I moved into a house alone.

I felt abandoned, rejected, unloved. I was having one big pity party. I was angry with everyone, but mostly with myself. I guess in some ways I was just afraid of the unknown. I felt myself pulling away from God, the church and my family. I had not done it physically, I was still going through the motions but my heart and mind just were not where they needed to be.

I am so glad that I did not stop my routine of church attendance. At the time it was only a routine for me. I did not know what else to do if I did not go to church. I knew that I did not want that old life of drinking and men hopping to return; but I did not know what I wanted or needed. One Sunday morning the choir sang a song I had never heard before, but it was what I needed at the time of my need. I still do not know the title of the song or the original artists. I only know the words that saved my life, renewed my mind and restored my heart. "I almost let go, but Jesus held me close and He wouldn't let go." I felt the tears stream down. I was so sorry for all the ill feelings and thoughts that I had. How could I have possibly allowed the enemy to pull me to this place of despair? I knew that with everything I had faced within that past year that Jesus was holding me tight and He had never let go! I was the first to bow down when the alter call was made and I was the last to get up.

It did not take long for me to enjoy living alone. Having privacy and quiet became quite nice. I could study without interruption. I could use the bathroom without someone barging in or knocking on the door before I finished. The telephone was always available when I wanted to use it. And, if I bought something and put it in the refrigerator just for me, when I went back to get it, it was always there. By September, I had settled in nicely.

In October, God had placed on the heart of the pastor and chairman deacon to have a month long revival. In preparation for the revival, as the Local Ministers' Council President, I called for a weeklong meeting for the ministers. The theme for the ministers for the year was, "Vessels of Honor Meet for the Master's Use" and it was what we would study during that week. As you might have guessed by now, it was once again meant for me. I came out of the week with more strength and determination than I had ever remembered having in my adult life and I have not looked back.

The revival was a success in more ways than you could ever imagine. God revealed some of the gifts that He had manifested on His people. Demons were cast out, souls were reclaimed and new souls were saved. People were healed and prophecies were fulfilled. (I'll get back to that in a moment). I did not miss a night. At the end of November, the Lord had placed it on the heart of the pastor to continue for one additional week. So for thirty-eight days straight, I was in church every night and I was abundantly blessed for the sacrifice.

Mid way through the revival, my great-uncle Jimmy started attending. Uncle Jimmy was a Baptist Minister that had been exposed to the doctrine of the Holy Ghost some years ago most likely from his youth. He rejoined the church and one evening he hugged me real tight and long after the altar prayer and whispered in my ear. He said, "Baby, God is going to deliver you before this revival is over." I really had no idea what he was referring to; perhaps he had heard my cries at the altar. I had a tendency to really moan and wail but not in agony, it was gratefulness.

I had completed my first year of probation on October 30th and when I received a telephone call from my probation officer in November I felt my heart fall to the floor. I could not imagine what I had done wrong. I knew that I had not missed any reporting dates and I had submitted all of the paperwork required. Why was she calling me? She had never called me in the entire year I had been reporting to her.

The conversations went something like this: "Wynette?" "Yes, speaking." "This is M.M." "Yes, I know who you are." "I have some news for you." "Okay?" "You have been released from probation; I am putting your papers in the mail today. You do not have to report anymore, you are free!" I shouted out without thought or apprehension, "Thank You, Jesus! Thank You, Jesus! Oh hallelujah, thank you, Jesus!" I had forgotten that I was at work and I heard her giggle on the other end of the phone, the joyous type not mockingly, and then she said, "Good Luck to you!" I did not need luck; I had Jesus!

CHAPTER THIRTY-ONE

I do not regret dedicating my life to God. Many people do not understand my focus. I do not expect them to. What God has for me, is for me. What He has for you is yours. We all have a purpose, God's plan for our lives. It is up to each of us to seek God to find what purpose He intends for us.

Do I have regrets? Yes, I regret exposing my children to my past. I regret not pursuing my educational aspirations. I regret not marrying my one true love when I had the opportunity. I regret the sins that pulled me away from God. I regret any hurt that I may have caused someone else, knowingly or unknowingly. I regret not telling those I love how much I love them. (I'm getting better with that one.) I regret not being as close to my daughter as I would like. I regret not seeking emotional help earlier in my life (although I may not have been receptive to it then). I regret pushing away those who genuinely loved me. I regret not always being the best example I should be. And, I regret the years I wasted exposing myself to the wiles of Satan when I could have been working for the Lord.

With all my regrets, I have so much more to be thankful for. For my life and my health, with all my ailments, I really do have reasonably good health. For shelter and security, I am thankful. I have a family that loves me unconditionally and that I love beyond what words could ever express. I have been blessed with friends … some have said that I use that word too lightly but I think not. Seven in the eyes of God is completion and I can think of seven people not including my family that God has allowed me to call friend. I will name them, but not in any order of importance because they are equally important in different ways. I have been blessed to call these people my friends:

Angela
Stephanie
Wanda
Toni
Gena
San
Fay

133

In my defense I would like to incorporate a saying that was forwarded to me via email. I do not know the original author but it clearly defines girlfriends. (Archie, you are in a boat by yourself, you know what your friendship means to me.)

GIRLFRIENDS

When I was little, I used to believe in the concept of one best friend, and then I started to become a woman. And then I found out that if you allow your heart to open up, God will show you the best in many friends.

One friend's best is needed when you're going through things with your man.

Another friend's best is needed when you're going through things with your momma. Another when you want to shop, share, heal, hurt, joke, or just be. One friend will say let's pray together, another let's cry together, another let's fight together, another let's walk away together... One friend will meet your spiritual need. Another your shoe fetish, another your love for movies, another will be with you in your season of confusion. Another will be your clarifier, another the wind beneath your wings... But what ever their assignment in your life, on whatever the occasion, on whatever the day, or where ever you need them to meet you with their gym shoes on and hair pulled back, or to hold you back from making a complete fool of yourself- those are your best friends. It may all be wrapped up in one woman, but for many it's wrapped up in several - one from 7th grade, one from high school, several from the college years, a couple from old jobs, several from church, on some days your mother, on others your sisters, and on some days it's the one that you needed just for that day or week that you needed someone with a fresh perspective, or the one who didn't know all your baggage, or the one who would just listen without judging...? Those are good girlfriends/best friends. Men are wonderful; husbands are excellent; boyfriends are awesome; male friends are priceless...but if you've ever had a real good girlfriend, then you know there's nothing like her!

Thank God for girlfriends, those who honor intimacy, those who hold trust, and those who just got your back when you feel like life is just too heavy! I thank God for you. The special bond we share, that's unique to us. The words we've shared. The prayers we've sent up. The laughs, the tears, the phone calls, the emails, the shopping, the movies, the lunches, the dinners, the late night talks, afternoon talks, the weekend talks, all the talking, talking, talking and the listening, listening, listening...So whether you've been there 20 minutes or 20 years, I love you!

For all the other women that I have called friend or sister (Marilyn) throughout my lifetime, please know that today, you are no less my friend.

My life is different now. My smile is no longer a mask although at times I may use it to mask my temporary pain. When I smile it is not because I have obtained or excelled or even made some great accomplishment. I smile because I know that no matter what may happen, no matter what accomplishments or failures, I am in the hands of God. "If God be for us, who can be against us?"

If you have a story to tell or if you are going through something, please be advised that if you have God on your side and you are living to please Him, the outcome is you WIN!

So smile, when you smile the whole world smiles with you, even if they have no idea what is behind the smile. You will always have the advantage of knowing that it is God's grace, mercy and undying love that radiates through your smile.

AFTERWORD

I just want to take the opportunity to say thanks to my lay-editors: Toni, Michelle, Stephanie and Gena. I must thank Dr. Pamala Murphy who encouraged me to put my story in writing and for her dedication to reading it. *Georgio Sabino III*, my photographer, cover designer and friend, what can I say? Thanks, just does not seem like enough!

To my church family, thank you for your support and encouragement and for putting up with me as I wrote. I know it wasn't always easy to deal with me, during the sad times. (I was reliving some things, I thought I would never address…but it worked out for my good.)

To my beloved children, I'm sorry if my story embarrasses you. I love you both, dearly! I just needed to tell my story in order to heal and unfortunately in some instances this included your stories as well.

To anyone that I may have hurt in my writings or in my living, please accept my sincerest apology from the depth of my heart. I do not wish to cause harm or pain. If I have done something knowingly or unknowingly, I am sorry.

To those out there that I have helped in some form or fashion, don't thank me…thank God, for without Him, I am nothing and can do nothing.

Most of all to my family and close friends that have loved me unconditionally, even when you did not understand me and maybe found it hard to like me, God Bless You and know that you are forever loved! (Marilyn, for your unconditional love and financial assistance, THANKS, bunches…you know I love you, girl!)

And last but not least, to all of you that have encouraged me to do this…. THANK YOU! AND…KEEP SMILING!!!

Wynette A. Bryant
Mother, Daughter, Sister, Friend
AKA: Ms. Nette, Nette & Sissy

Life With A Smile